MW00460105

DRAWING
NEAR

GETTING TO KNOW

the God

WHO INTIMATELY

Knows You

PATRICIA
WHEATON

HiGHERLIFE
PUBLISHING & MARKETING

Drawing Near

Published by HigherLife Development Services Inc.
PO Box 623307
Oviedo, Florida 32762
www.ahigherlife.com

ISBN: 978-1-951492-43-4 PB
ISBN: 978-1-951492-44-1 EPub

Cover photo of Sinai: Photo 18972381 © Irochka | Dreamstime.com

10 9 8 7 6 5 4 3 2 1
Printed in the United States of America

DEDICATION

I would be so negligent if I didn't make known the sure faith my children have in God, and their continual faith in me. They have been diligent to affirm the True God. Their faith in me has been a great encouragement to me and has always energized me to fulfill my calling. I love you, Denard and Latisha, Eric and Carol, Kalaun and Tisa, Erica, and my grandchildren in a big way. I have been very desirous to see you walk into the greater things of God. There is always so much more to attain in our relationship with God; this is where our true purpose is found. I am an elated mother and grandmother and so proud of all that God has accomplished in you. A trillion times I say thank you for your love, what you have been and done for me. You are so dearly loved and appreciated by me, your Mom.

ACKNOWLEDGMENTS

I want to acknowledge first and foremost the Holy Spirit, who was truly the inspiration for this book. I had no idea I was writing a book, just journaling inspirational thoughts and words from the Holy Spirit, so amazing is He. I also want to acknowledge Dennis Anderson and Porche Mendez for their typing skills as I began to mold my ideas into a book. Thank you ever so much. Sherita West was one of the first members of New Life Church, and indeed I bless her for being willing to proofread my manuscript. You know you are loved. I want to acknowledge my children for eventually recognizing I needed quantity and quality time with God, and the great sacrifice they made. I love you in a big way. I acknowledge New Life Christian Church, which has been an active participant with me in a quest for more of Him, for all reasons and at all times. Truly this has helped to make it easy to seek for Greater Dimension in Christ and Higher Realms in His Presence. You are loved and so appreciated. I dearly want to acknowledge Pastors John and Beverly Heary. They read through the manuscript and praised it very highly. Pastor John did some necessary editing; Pastor Beverly read for the enjoyment of reading and for my support. She said that as she read, many times she would put the manuscript down because of the pleasure of His Presence entering in, causing her to meditate on what she had just read. This indeed made me know the Holy Spirit was inspirational in releasing His Presence. You two are so dear to my heart. I humbly acknowledge "No man is an island" and I give my gratitude to you all.

CONTENTS

INTRODUCTION

"If then you have been raised with Christ [to a new life, thus sharing His resurrection from the dead], aim at and seek the [rich, eternal treasures] that are above, where Christ is, seated at the right hand of God. And set your minds and keep them set on what is above (the higher things), not on the things that are on the earth. For [as far as this world is concerned] you have died, and your [new, real] life is hidden with Christ in God."
– Colossians 3:1-3 AMP

D o you desire *more* in your Christian experience? Do you feel a need for a more personal relationship with God?

Many Christians think that finding intimacy with God is a complicated process. It is not. In Him, you will find simplicity. In an intimate relationship with God, you will find the *more* you are looking for.

This book is written to lead you into a real relationship with God, one that is attained simply, one which can be achieved if you genuinely desire it. It contains insights gained through my own journey of seeking intimacy with God, because I, too, know what it is like to seek for fulfillment in other things without finding it.

For as long as I can remember, I had busied myself with the things of this world. Striving to maintain the accepted social standards kept me occupied. I had to go to all the right places, shows, concerts, restaurants, and wear the clothes which had the seal of social acceptance. Social standards that would mark me as someone special were a must. These things were sure to open doors in the world. I believe that there is an overwhelming tendency to get lost in the mundane of this world and not know it. I was lost, bewildered, and I was always striving, without knowing it.

I wanted to make my life what I wanted and hoped for. I really didn't have great dreams as some do. I wanted the normal – a husband, children, home, car, and a job as a teacher. I attained a husband, and wonderful children. I had a nice home and drove my Volvo from the showroom floor. I made good money on my job. The thing that was missing in my life was a relationship with Jesus. As life went on, I found myself divorced. Thinking I needed a good man, I went in search for one. I thought maybe it was more money I needed. I tried new and better houses. I returned to school at New Mexico State for my credentials. These things were what I wanted, but they proved not to be the answer. God will set us up and lead and draw us into His arms, and He surely did that for me. He let me get frustrated with my own abilities and I began to cry out to God, who I had only heard of occasionally from my mother and from occasional childhood Sunday school attendance. I was crying out for Him with a serious and genuine heart. "And it shall be that whoever shall call upon the name of the Lord (invoking, adoring, and worshipping the Lord-Christ) shall be saved" (Acts 2:21 AMP).

One day at work, it seemed like everything faded away but His voice; I was aware of no one, just His voice. He came to me and I knew it was Him. He asked me if I wanted to come with Him and I said, "YES." I knew that I immediately had to follow and obey. I followed Him and was baptized in that life-giving Name of Jesus for the remission of my sins, and I received the Holy Spirit. I remember crying so hard in repentance from my sin; it was godly sorrow for who I had been, which will always bring forth fruits of repentance to God's Glory. "If you have really turned from your sins to God, you'll produce fruit that will prove it automatically" (Matt. 3:8 CJB). God delivered my mind from the bondage I had put myself in, and He introduced me to a personal, intimate relationship with Him. I accepted all He offered me and through this I acquired a life of peace, joy and righteousness in the Holy Ghost. Oh! The wholeness and completeness I experience every day! This does not mean I do not have tests and trials, but it does mean that I have received the Truth (Word) that keeps me firmly established in Him (Truth). My circumstances do not determine my fullness or my completeness; my living in and through His Truth and Presence is my completeness. Now, I seek with my whole heart the things that are above. I take ample time to enjoy and relate to my given position in heavenly places; my Heavenly preoccupation determines my value to God on this earth. Many say you can be so heavenly-minded that you are no earthly good, but I say just the opposite: You can be so earthly-minded that you are no heavenly good. After all, according to Jesus, it is the heavenly kingdom that must be established on earth. "We pray that Your kingdom will come—that what You want will be done here on earth, the same as in heaven" (Matt. 6:10 ERV). As God showed Moses and others, it is only His heavenly pattern that can please Him.

How can one ever find the Heavenly Places, the Presence of God, and receive its pleasure? In one of his writings St. Augustine says, "Your affections are the steps. Your will is the way. By loving, you ascend. By neglecting, you descend. For the heart is not raised as the body is raised. For the body to be raised it needs to change place. For the heart to be raised, it needs only to change its desire." Today, start this exercise; set your affection on Him and the things of Heaven. Be willing to eliminate everything that hinders your heart's flow to Him, re-adjust things that are a "must," and put "out of order" anything that intrudes upon your precious time with God. God has promised that those who seek will find.

This book is written to help you find intimacy with God. It is full of the precious moments and the special times I have spent in one-on-one conversation, musing and pondering in His Presence. Enjoy the many quotes from my favorite authors, such as A.W. Tozer and F.B. Meyer, that will help you discern His Presence. One of my greatest desires is that the whole Church may know and seek what is so richly available to us – the awareness of living in Heavenly Places in His Presence. "That is, God raised us with the Messiah Yeshua and seated us with Him in heaven, in order to exhibit in the ages to come how infinitely rich is His grace, how great is His kindness toward us who are united with the Messiah Yeshua" (Eph. 2:6 CJB).

I once had a dream in which I was upstairs in the master bedroom and my husband came in with a group of people and began to show them around our room. I was upset with him for doing this; this room was personal between him and me, but he didn't seem to mind and continued the tour. I eventually accepted it, then I awoke. I understood the dream, but could not place why I had it until I began to compile my journal. Then the Lord brought back this dream and told me He wanted me to make some of it into a book about His intimate Presence. Some who have not known intimacy with the Lord possibly will not enjoy it and think it is too mushy, but if you'll spend time in God's Presence and desire intimacy with Him, you will soon understand it. Relationship brings intimacy, intimacy brings revelation, and revelation will bring even greater and deeper intimacy.

You might finish this book quickly, but afterwards, go back and take time with the many truths that I pray will inspire your heart. There are 52 weeks in a year, so you can take ample time to meditate, memorize and journal to retain what you receive and to increase your fellowship with the Person of our Lord through the Holy Spirit, which will last you a lifetime.

A special note to men: Some will start reading this book and believe its only appeal is to women, but everything in this book follows after the heart of the patriarch David. The scripture says he was indeed a man after God's own heart. Our society has distracted men from praying and entering into intimate relationship with the Lord. Society puts labels on men who fall deeply and intimately in love with the Lord. In the scriptures we find that most of the notable prayers and intimate fellowship were experienced by men, especially David the giant killer. David was as macho as you can get; he fought with the lion and a bear, and the women adored him, but he had deep intimacy with the Lord. "My soul longeth yea, even fainteth for the courts of the Lord: my heart and my flesh crieth out for the living God" (Ps. 84:2 KJV). "As the hart pants and longs for the water brooks, so I pant and long for You, O God. My inner self thirsts for God, for the Living God. When shall I come and behold the face of God?" (Ps. 42:1-2 AMPC). David's macho nature did not hinder his intimate desire for His God; yours shouldn't either. I challenge men not to take your identity from the world's concept of a man, but to let God define you as men after His own heart. Men and women alike, please enjoy yourselves! *Bon appetit!*

TODAY

Today is the first day of the rest of my life. The first speaks of new beginnings. Lord, since this is the first day of the rest of my life, I know it is of the utmost importance what I do with this day You have given me. I choose to start this day with those things that help to direct my life and hold me in Your Presence. Then I choose to recall throughout the day this remembrance of You, and not just a happenstance thought of You, but a deep breathing in of Your Presence. I read that we should start each day in Your face, then go face the world. Today I need Your wisdom and Your righteousness and Your sanctification. Today I need Your grace more than ever. Today, Lord, I need, for my own good, to be faithful to the time I give You; completely attentive to You. The time I have devoted to give You is filled with an all-out zealous desire to know You and to attain to Your Presence. We are to lead sacrificial lives, that yield and give up something that they desire for self, such as time, money, and ambition if needed, for today is a day I move closer to You. I will draw nigh to You for You have promised to indeed draw nigh to me. I do

I do not want to wake tomorrow and feel that I wasted precious time in my quest to know You more perfectly.

not want to wake tomorrow and feel that I wasted precious time in my quest to know You more perfectly. The nominal way most people believe sufficient to know You is far removed from Paul's admonishment that we should count all things as dung just to know You (Phil. 3:8). We read, pray, and muse on Your Wonderful Person in Your Word. I earnestly feel attached to You in this time of devotion and worship; You saturate and surround me with You. It might necessitate early rising to start my day with You, and there are all sorts of things and people I might have to cut short or cut out. I have experienced the solitary times, but never am I really alone. You are worth everything I sacrifice. This is the only way I must start my today, for every new day continues to be the first day of the rest of my life, that can only prosper by keeping You first and primary every day.

SCRIPTURE FOR MEDITATION:

"And in the morning, rising up a great while before day, he went out, and departed into a solitary place, and there prayed" (Mark 1:35 KJV).

WORD FOR THOUGHT:

Solitary *– alone, without companions, or unattended. Living alone or avoiding the society of others; be the only one or ones (Pey, 1977, p. 924).*

MEDITATE ON:

Every day is the beginning day of the rest of your life, and starting each day with Him affirms your dependence on His Presence in your life. Oh, how I need you, Lord!

RELATIVE PRAYER:

Lord, You are my number One, my First; keep me always needing You and wanting to have time alone with just You. Lord you told David to seek your face, and he replied, "Lord I will seek Your face." I want to start my new day in Your face. Face to face.

JOURNAL
A Reflection of Your Thoughts

_____

_____

_____

_____

_____

WEEK TWO

FOCUS

Lord, my desire, need, aspiration and all my thoughts have radically changed. My thoughts are filled with what You are thinking, what You want, and what pleases You today. It is the constant need to want Your pleasure in my life that keeps me focused. If we do not learn to focus on You the Holy Ghost will never be able to send a clear image of Your Person. When we focus, there is a conveyance of Your attributes presented to us continually until we behold Your likeness. This is on-going, for we know that Your Person can never be exhausted. I imagine that beholding the fullness of Your Person would be mind-blowing, astonishing, amazing and awe-inspiring above all else. I think of the wonderment and amazement Moses must have experienced. This keeps me assiduous in my quest to stay focused. Can I tell You, Lord, I am having fun and I am more satisfied then ever? I am a treasure hunter on a quest to find riches. Everything I find about Your Person and Your ways rejoices my heart like nothing else can. W.O.W, Wonder of Wonders, I understand David when he admonished us, "taste and see that the Lord is good: blessed is the man that trusteth in Him" (Ps. 34:8 KJV). My focus is insistent, demanding clarity of Your Image. There will always be things to distract us, but

> *My focus is insistent, demanding clarity of Your Image.*

I believe the greater our desire and need for Him, and the greater our joy in having Him as our main attraction, so will our hearts continually be directed toward Him. "So will not we go back from thee: quicken us, and we will call upon thy Name" (Ps. 80:18 KJV). The Holy Spirit in His quickening power *will indeed call you back to focus on the beautiful face He is revealing to you. He* will usher us again and again, bringing our focus back to His face, and it will become our life occupation. "When the Lord calls us to Himself, He calls us to an eternal occupation" (A.W. Tozer).

SCRIPTURE FOR MEDITATION:

"Only be thou strong and very courageous, that thou mayest observe to do according to all the law, which Moses My servant commanded thee: turn not from it to the right hand or to the left, that thou mayest prosper whithersoever thou goest" (Joshua 1:7 KJV).

WORD FOR THOUGHT:

"Assiduous": Constant in application; attentive; industrious; devoted; persevering; unremitting; performed with constant diligence or attention (The Living Webster Dict., p. 60).

MEDITATE ON:

Think on the Holy Spirit that quickens (makes alive) your spirit, keeping you attentive, unremitting and devout to your quest to behold His face, His Person. Listen often to the song "Show Me Your face." There are many renditions of the song, but I believe Juanita Bynum's was the first. We should all think on and be more sensitive to the Holy Spirit, for we do adore the Holy Spirit's revealing Presence in our lives.

RELATIVE PRAYER:

Lord, that I may be focused, to behold and receive the satisfaction found in You. Lord, I command my eyes to be set as a flint on You. Lord, "I set my face like a flint, confident that I'll never regret this" (Is. 50:7 MSG). So we will not go back from You, quicken us Lord and we will call upon Your Name.

JOURNAL
A REFLECTION OF YOUR THOUGHTS

_____

_____

_____

_____

WOW!

Wow! Just being away with Jesus this week was full of inspiration and conversation. The love of God is so perfect. If you find this place of His all-consuming Love, nothing but Him will really matter. If you find this place many external things will not matter like they did at one time; I want you to believe this. You will know that it is not about being important to man. You will know it is not about who recognizes you. When you desire, and this becomes your greatest desire, to be recognized and important to Him, He crowds you and can fill you to capacity until you recognize there is no place left even for yourself. He wants no sign of the old you, but you inundated with only Him. Wow! Him living on the inside with His all-consuming love is a thought you relish, for He has so much He wants to do with your life. The Lord spoke to me during this break away and said that when I have Him right, I will be exuberant with His virtue and overflowing with His Presence. Lord, I understand you want me to know You are my wealth and worth; my best times are when You lavish me profusely with Yourself. This place of consuming Love and Presence is why just the shadow of Peter could heal the sick without him touching anyone. This virtue permeated the handkerchiefs from the body of Paul. Remember how virtue bounced off Jesus? It was in the wings of His prayer shawl. He imparts to us His virtue, love, and Presence as we spend time with Him. I do not believe anything can take the place of time well spent with Him, not theology of scripture or giving of your finances; nothing else can produce this copious virtue. This virtue you do not readily see, but it is something that is felt and becomes tangible on the object it touches or even comes close to. You do not have to feel this, but most of the time when this virtue is present, I feel it tangibly on my hands and many times every cell in my body seems to be vibrating. The Lord has many ways to make you know that His virtue is with you to heal and deliver. There are times that I actually know He has taken control of my eyes and mouth. I sense Him seeing through me and speaking for me.

He imparts to us His virtue, love, and Presence as we spend time with Him.

Wow! What an extraordinary, supernatural feeling. The actuality and reality of our Lord is to be desired more than anything. WOW! Wonder of Wonders!

SCRIPTURE FOR MEDITATION:

"But when He, Who had chosen and set me apart [even] before I was born and had called me by His grace (His undeserved favor and blessing), saw fit and was pleased to reveal (unveil, disclose) His Son within me so that I might proclaim Him among the Gentiles (the non-Jewish world) as the glad tidings (Gospel), immediately I did not confer with flesh and blood [did not consult or counsel with any frail human being or communicate with anyone]. Nor did I [even] go up to Jerusalem to those who were apostles (special messengers of Christ) before I was, but I went away and retired into Arabia, and afterward I came back again to Damascus" (Galatians 1:15-17 AMP).

WORD FOR THOUGHT:

Virtue:
- *Dunamis - force (literally or figuratively); specif. miraculous power (usually by implication, a miracle itself) — ability, abundance, meaning, might(-ily, -y, -y deed), (worker of) miracle(-s), power, strength, violence, mighty (wonderful) work* (Strong's Conc. #1411).
- *Dunamai — to be powerful, able. Of uncertain affinity; to be able or possible—be able, can, could, may, might, be possible, and be of power* (Strong's Conc. #1410).

MEDITATE ON:

Think on a love that fills you to capacity until you can't distinguish you in operation, and your existence is but naught; a love that overwhelms and transposes you into just One and fills you with the power of that One.

RELATIVE PRAYER:

O Lord, Paul says, "For me to live is Christ" (Phil. 1:21). He knew he was on a mission, and he also knew to accomplish his call he had to live in You and through You. Holy Spirit, as we remember this, we know You will finish what You have started in us for only You can secure this place for us.

JOURNAL

A Reflection of Your Thoughts

_____

_____

_____

_____

_____

_____

_____

_____

_____

_____

_____

_____

_____

_____

_____

_____

_____

_____

_____

_____

_____

UNCLOTHED

There are times when I feel a loss of Your Presence and feel unclothed. I say unclothed, because Your Presence has become as necessary to me as the clothes I wear. I feel my nakedness with a longing to be clothed with You, for my awareness of You is an essential part of my grooming. I feel perplexed, and I wonder and search myself to make sure I have not done anything that would displease You, anything that would cause You to depart from my presence for a while. I feel like a blind person groping and feeling for the One my soul loves. My heart reaches out to touch and feel the One who clothes me with Himself. Recording artist Grace Williams says, "Just want to be with You; as the waters need the sea." I remember the day I was listening to this song and I heard You tell me just like the waters need the sea, know that the sea also needs the water. Without the waters the sea would have a vast emptiness. The water and the sea belong to each other for eternity. Oh, how beautifully You whisper Your intimate love for me. When I look upon the ocean I know this is truth seen in nature, and I see eternity in it. Could it be possible that Your desire for us is as vast as our need for You? For we have concluded that we be (exist, live, happen, occur) nothing without You. Without the clothing of Your Presence, there would be a need to hide myself in what would become a dark, cold place; I already know the confusion this place would bring. It is Your Presence that brings light, brilliance, and warmth to my life: the place of peace and freedom from a guilty conscience. No matter what we try to invent

> *Could it be possible that Your desire for us is as vast as our need for You?*

to camouflage the absence of Your Presence, it will not be sufficient. Is it possible that Adam and Eve first felt their nakedness, not being clothed with His glory, because they lost the very Presence of His Holiness? I need You surrounding me. I need to be wrapped and clothed in You; I have no holiness, no righteousness but that You graciously impart into us royally. "Because of Him, you are in Messiah Yeshua, Who was made to us wisdom from God, and righteousness and sanctification, and redemption, that, as it is written, 'He who boasts, let him boast in the Lord'" (I Cor. 1:30, 31 WMB). This way of life is my ultimate desire. Oh! Oblige me, O Lord! Clothe me, Lord, with Yourself and in full pleasure I will be satisfied.

SCRIPTURE FOR MEDITATION:

"Then the eyes of them both were opened, and they knew that they were naked; and they sewed fig leaves together and made themselves apron-like girdles. And they heard the sound of the Lord God walking in the garden in the cool of the day, and Adam and his wife hid themselves from the presence of the Lord God among the trees of the garden" *(Genesis 3:7-8 AMP).*

WORD FOR THOUGHT:

Ultimate *– Farthest … extreme; last as in a series; coming at the end, as of a course of action or a process; coming as a final result; final and decisive; as an ultimate check to progress; forming a final claim or object; His ultimate goal or purpose … the final point; the final result; the conclusion … (Pey, 1977, p. 1071).*

MEDITATE ON:

Where is the finishing place for you? What is the finale? At the end, is your ultimate hope to be clothed totally with the Person of Christ? To be covered again in His Presence (glory) as Adam and Eve were in the beginning, causing all to fall short of His glory (Romans 3:23).

RELATIVE PRAYER:

Lord I long to be clothed with You by regeneration and renewing, which is the work of the Holy Spirit. It is the Holy Spirit's mission to bring us to the place of our nativity in full acceptance once again, and I thank you for the process (Titus 3:5-6).

JOURNAL
A Reflection of Your Thoughts

FALLING IN LOVE

Falling in love with Jesus is by far the best thing I have ever done. The places I have gone, the people I've met and the things I have done have all been profitable, but there is only one thing that is pronounced as best; and falling in love with Jesus holds that title. Those who fall "head over heels" in love with Him become totally surrendered to Him. You are His "doulos" (love slave) and to fulfill His wants is the joy of your life, for all you want is to be with Him. Just let Him show you through a dream, vision, word or experience that He is thinking of you. The experience carries its weight in gold; you are compelled to simply surrender your heart to Him again and again at His every command.

Those who have fallen in love with Jesus have the characteristics of the man Joshua, who went to the Tent of Meeting with Moses, but after Moses left, he still had a desire to linger in the Presence of the Lord. Those who love Him that way and linger at the Tent of Meeting (Presence) can expect greater revelation. They can expect to attain higher heights and deeper depths in Him.

I remember the first real vow I made to the Lord. It was a prayer vow to spend a certain amount of time every day in His Presence. It was a one-on-One encounter with Him. When the year was over, the Lord gave me an experience in the Spirit in which I was zoomed up to the Heavenlies and was amazed by how high He took me. It was an out-of-body experience and every part of me went with the Lord. He took me above the world and stars and He then brought me to the depths of the ocean where the water trickled up from the floor. Then I heard Him tell me (in my spirit) of the deeper depths and higher heights. I truly sensed He was smiling at me, and I saw His hand, indeed a big hand. He was taking joy that

He could reveal this to me. Oh, the secret things God wants to show us of His power and greatness. "Call to me and I will answer you, and tell you [and even show you] great and mighty things, [things which have been confined and hidden], which you do not know and understand and cannot distinguish" (Jer. 33:3 AMP). "Judah, pray to Me, and I will answer you. I will tell you important secrets. You have never heard these things before" (ERV).

Joshua was a faithful and obedient servant to Moses, but He was not looking for "brownie points." Rather, he desired the Presence of God. You must make sure your motives are right. Never seek God to earn recognition from others, just from Him; in fact, your desire is to know He is smiling on you and your pursuit of Him is enticing Him to draw you closer and closer. When there is true love, service is no longer service. It becomes your privilege and honor to Him. Don't allow your time with Him to be all about your promotion, your gifts, but rather about your desire to love Him much more than you do right now. Falling in love with Jesus is the best thing you can do for yourself in this life. Not only does it avail you with the great privilege of being close to Him (Presence), but it also brings many fringe benefits. I believe that every cell in your body responds to a love relationship with Yeshua.

> *When there is true love, service is no longer service. It becomes your privilege and honor to Him.*

SCRIPTURE FOR MEDITATION:

"And Jacob served seven years for Rachel; and they seemed to him but a few days because of the love he had for her" (Genesis 29:20 AMP).

WORD FOR THOUGHT:

Servant – *The New Testament uses a Greek word for the term servant, "doulos," which gives us a very good word picture of a servant heart. Generally "doulos" signifies bondage, but most commonly applies to a servant who has willingly bonded himself to a master. In essence, "doulos" means, "because it is well with me as your slave, and because I love you and your household (kingdom), I will serve you forever on the basis of my deep love for you" (Damazio, 1996, p. 83).*

MEDITATE ON:

Being a reflection of a love slave, "doulos." We can't ascertain how deep and how wide His love is for us, no matter how we try, but reflect on how deep your love flows for Him. Can certain situations or circumstances negate any portion of your love for Him? Think of our brother Paul and all he went through and note in your heart that at the end of his life, he seemed to be more surrendered to be a servant and more in love than ever before.

RELATIVE PRAYER:

Pray that your love for Him will become the true motivation for your serving Him.

JOURNAL
A REFLECTION OF YOUR THOUGHTS

THANKFUL

Our thankfulness is the first key to accessing the Holy of Holies ("Shekinah"). Upon entering we must reminisce and avail ourselves of true thankfulness. There are some mornings I awake with this spirit of abundant thanks gushing through and from me. (I will not tell you that some mornings He, the Holy Spirit, reminds me that regardless of what I feel, I am indeed thankful.) I awake and fill my mouth with thankfulness every morning, but there are times that exceed the normal. I awake always thankful for my life, health, and strength of body. If you have ever been really sick, you know this is not just a cliché. I am thankful for salvation and the Precious gift of the Holy Ghost. It is God who sent His Son in the flesh to do for me what I could not do for myself. I am thankful that I live in this nation with all its wonderful conveniences. I am thankful for this body of believers, able to pray in His Great Name

> **Never resist the prompting to give abundant thanks.**

and see things happen, and so much more; but there are abundant times of thankfulness that seem to flow from the joy of my relationship with Him – that I know Him and know He is responsive to me. These are the times that I get beside myself in thanksgiving; just knowing He is responsive to me. "I look up at Your macro-skies, dark and enormous, Your handmade sky-jewelry, moon and stars mounted in their settings. Then I look at my micro-self and wonder, Why do You bother with us? Why take a second look our way?" (Psalm 8:3-4 MSG).

I am so thankful that I did not settle for just being a churchgoer or "churchee."

I am so thankful that I listened to the Holy Spirit when He told me there was so much more. Believe me, every experience God allows you raises the gauge of thankfulness. Thankfulness is something we do to express our gratitude and we can do it in many ways. We should know out of all the people who deserve our thanks no one compares to our God, plus thankfulness to Him leads to greater places in Him. According to Psalms 100, we enter into the gates with thanksgiving on our way to the Holy of Holies (Shekinah). Never resist the prompting to give abundant thanks, for it is He (Holy Spirit) who is bidding you to draw nigh, ultimately to the place of His Glory (Shekinah), the place where the Cherubim dwell. There He will meet with you.

SCRIPTURE FOR MEDITATION:

"There I will meet with you and, from above the Mercy Seat, from between the two Cherubim that are upon the ark of the Testimony, I will speak intimately with you of all which I will give you in commandment to the Israelites" (Exodus 25:22 AMP).

WORD FOR THOUGHT:

Gushing – *To pour, to rush forth, as a fluid from confinement; to flow suddenly or copiously; to be extravagantly and effusively sentimental … (Pey, 1977, p. 431).*

MEDITATE ON:

Our path to the Holy of Holies (Shekinah). This is the Pattern of God: the outer court (thanksgiving), the inner court (praise), and the Holy of Holies (worship). When thankfulness is gushing, you ascend in your progression into the Holy of Holies (Shekinah Presence).

RELATIVE PRAYER:

We ask the Holy Spirit to flood our remembrance with reason to be thankful. We ask Him to release into our thoughts remembrance until we enter into the overflow of thankfulness and praise and on to His Glory. Lord we believe Your Word that we will see Your glory.

JOURNAL
A REFLECTION OF YOUR THOUGHTS

A STORYBOOK ENDING

The deeper we go in Your Presence, the greater love we find. To truly express this Love in writing is not even possible. This Love You give us must be experienced to be defined. Your Love is the kind of love that is only possible in storybooks, but it far excels storybook love. It is the kind of Love we always wanted to find, but with everything we have seen, thought it was nowhere to be found.

Lord, You are my Prince Charming and I truly see You as the all-together Lovely One, the Rose of Sharon, and there is nothing that shines brighter than You in my heart and life. Oh! Lord, You keep taking me deeper and deeper into Your Love. Truly with every encounter I want to go deeper still, deeper than I have ever gone before. I recall when I had only been a Christian about a year. I was lying in bed about to go to sleep. It was on a Sunday after church (The Lord's Day). I was being very thankful about several things, especially about being a Christian. I was praising You from the depths of my heart and I slipped into a place of worth-ship. I really did not even know it was possible. It seemed to me that I entered into a state or a place, The Presence of Love that far exceeds anything I had ever come in contact with before. It was, can I say, inclusive of every love I have experienced. The feeling is one of insurmountably having all you need to thrive for eternity. I began to express myself in delight for an experience that only He could give. I knew this was the tangible Love of Jesus, so all encompassing.

As a little girl I remember loving all the storybook endings, which leave you with the greatest pleasure. You could lie down and go to sleep with happy thoughts, believing everything in your life is meant to end well. God calls us His beloved and He will never forget His responsibility for us. "This is God's Word on the subject: 'As soon as Babylon's seventy years are up and not a day before, I'll show up and take care of you as I promised and bring you back home. I know what I'm doing. I have it all planned out—plans to take care of you, not abandon you, plans to give you the future you hope for'" (Jer. 29:10-11 MSG). "I say this because I know the plans that I have for you." This message is from the Lord. "I have good plans for you. I don't plan to hurt you. I plan to give you hope and a good future" (ERV). Lord, I know that as I love You and seek Your face with every part of my being, I believe I will have that storybook ending, "And they lived happily ever after," a real ending to the most precious thing we have, life. I am convinced, because nothing is bigger or greater, nothing compares to Your love. This is the greatest love story ever told and why shouldn't it be? This is God's Love Story. You are the true Prince Charming (Hero).

> *This is the greatest love story ever told and why shouldn't it be? This is God's Love Story.*

SCRIPTURE FOR MEDITATION:

"For I am persuaded beyond doubt (am sure) that neither death, nor life, nor angels, nor principalities, nor things impending and threatening nor things to come, nor powers, nor height, nor depth, nor anything else in all creation will be able to separate us from the love of God which is in Christ Jesus our Lord" (Romans 8:38-39 AMP).

"I'm absolutely convinced that nothing—nothing living or dead, angelic or demonic, today or tomorrow, high or low, thinkable or unthinkable—absolutely nothing can get between us and God's love because of the way that Jesus our Master has embraced us" (MSG).

WORD FOR THOUGHT:

Insurmountable – impossible to overcome: incapable of being surmounted, overcome, passed over, or solved (Merriam-Webster).

MEDITATE ON:

Deeply falling into His insurmountable Love. Experiencing His Love to the degree that it permeates your being so that even your smile and words invite others to seek and know His Love. In the Song of Solomon the virgins come and ask the Shulamite how her Beloved is better than others. She answers by describing what she knows about Him; "His words are sweetness itself; He is altogether desirable. This is my darling, and this is my Friend, daughter of Yerushalayim" (SOS 5:16 CJB). "Yes, women of Jerusalem, my lover is everything I desire. His mouth is the sweetest of all. This is my lover; this is my darling" (ERV).

RELATIVE PRAYER:

I pray to be flooded and filled with this insurmountable Love. I pray that He will increase my awareness of His Love. Lord, you know I love You and I want to feel Your tangible embrace often, for You are everything anyone should desire.

JOURNAL
A REFLECTION OF YOUR THOUGHTS

AUTHOR AND FINISHER

Tere are times, and most likely there will always be those times when I feel my worthlessness. Times when my biggest complaint is me, myself and I. The times you feel you have wasted too much time, missed too many opportunities and left a host of things unfinished; you feel undone in your thoughts. That is the time to quickly seek the Lord and find His Presence. No amount of doing can suffice to remedy this condition or state of mind. This state of mind is about self and what you have been able to do or not do. The prime place for our worthless feeling is in His Presence, as we come in so lowly, knowing He will lift us up and define our person in Him. "And those whom He thus foreordained, He also called; and those whom He called He also justified (acquitted, made righteous, putting them into right standing with Himself). And those whom He justified, He also glorified [raising them to a heavenly dignity and condition or state of being.] What then shall we say to [all] this? If God is for us, who can [be] against us? [Who can be our foe, if God is on our side?]" (Rom. 8: 30-31 AMPC). He is the Author and Finisher of our faith. You are His plan; I am His plan. We make sense to Him if not to anyone else; we must let Him be our consummator.

In this book of Romans, Paul ventures to say that he dare not judge himself, this belongs to God and only Him. We are to take the Word and examine ourselves, some of the things we see make us want to address the situation with a whip, but hear me; take it into His Presence. Sometimes we deal with what we see with pity and want to sink into a depressed and weary place; but take it into His Presence. There only will you understand the way of the Lord.

I once had a dream and in it I was doing something that I thought was godly, but in the dream, the Lord made me to know it was not of Him and in the next scene of the dream I was in a shower. There were other people in this shower. Showers or baths in a dream can represent the cleansing power of the Holy Spirit. When I awoke, I realized God had already washed me from my failure as He does with all His beloved. Wow! God is an excellent consummator. Let Him speak to you of your worth. Get right up under His wing and let Him touch you in a way that will make you know you matter. Know that His plan is working, for you mean so very much to Him in this age and the one to come. Our worth has already been established in Him and His heart.

The prime place for our worthless feeling is in His Presence, as we come in so lowly, knowing He will lift us up and define our person in Him.

He does not rely on our opinion of our self, or anyone else's opinion. He says, "I will never leave you or forsake you" (Heb. 13:5 KJV). "I am sure of this: that the One Who began a good work among you will keep it growing until it is completed on the Day of the Messiah Yeshua" (Phil. 1:6 CJB). Keep yourself in the Presence and hands of the Finisher of our faith.

SCRIPTURE FOR MEDITATION:

"Therefore leaving the principles of the doctrine of Christ, let us go on unto perfection …" (Hebrews 6:1 KJV). Therefore let us go on and get past the elementary stage in the teachings and doctrine of Christ (the Messiah), advancing steadily toward the completeness and perfection that belong to spiritual maturity …" (AMP).

WORD FOR THOUGHT:

Consummator – (one who) makes (something) perfect or complete, is highly expert; one who fulfills in every detail, is extremely skilled and accomplished; one who makes a marriage (via intercourse) (adapted from Webster, New World).

MEDITATE ON:

In Hebrews the sixth chapter and the first verse, we are being admonished to go on into our Perfection in our Consummator. We dare not rely on ourselves. It is only as we live in Him, through Him, and from Him that God's finished product, His plan for our lives, can come into view.

RELATIVE PRAYER:

Lord our Father, we believe that Jesus is our Consummator. Give us grace to be yielded to the Holy Spirit in all things. We know, God, that you never intended for us to finish the book of our lives when we did not author it.

JOURNAL
A REFLECTION OF YOUR THOUGHTS

_____

_____

_____

_____

_____

_____

_____

_____

_____

_____

_____

_____

_____

_____

SHOW ME YOUR GLORY

Lord, as I lie here, I think of the testimonies of Your Glory. I realize that when we confess that we are seeking Your Face, we are really reaching for testaments of Your Glory, a revelation of Your Person. All through the scriptures, You reveal the testaments that bring Glory to Your Name. We can see your glorious Face through these testaments. You called Moses to be a testament of Your Glory, and surely he was. Shadrach, Meshach, and Abednego were outrageous testaments of Your Glory. Space will not allow us to try to mention all these faithful witnesses, as the Book of Hebrews tells us. These testaments are revelatory and show the awe of Your Divine Person. We are amazed as we behold the infinitude of Your abilities in every situation. As I lie here motionless in body, my spirit is reaching into Your realms of glory, desiring and longing for more. Reaching for Glory that I know is inexhaustible to all of us. The amazing displays of the testament of Glory can only be known by You, and only belong to You. I was watching the news the other day and heard the newscaster say scientists had located another galaxy with thousands of planets. Lord, this is all about Your Glory and it is so vast.

I believe the days are drawing nigh, and we are now at the threshold of the greatest manifestation of testimonies to Your Glory. It will break out all over this world. I truly believe Lord, You have saved the best for last; the church that was purchased with the Precious Blood of Jesus Christ has Glory to reveal that the world won't be able to believe. "The silver is mine, and the gold is mine, saith the Lord of hosts. The glory of this latter house shall be greater than of the former, saith the Lord of hosts: and in this place will I give peace, saith the Lord of Hosts" (Haggai 2:8-9 KJV). "I own the silver, I own the gold! Decree of the God-of-the-Angel-Armies. This Temple is going to end up far better than it started out, a glorious beginning but and even more glorious finish: a place in which I will hand out wholeness and holiness! Decree of God-of-the-Angel-Armies" (MSG). The latter and former rains are

When people see the Jesus of the Word, the multitude will want to follow Him into His Kingdom.

descending full of Your Glory. This will include anointing and mantles of years past that will be revived with this glorious latter house. Leaders of churches believed that when we showed the world that we could keep up with it in the financial arena Christ would be glorified. I agree that churches must be good stewards of His finances, but this focus has caused the church to lose its place. This was not because of monies, but because in many

cases the church's focus shifted from the face of the Lord. Glory is the pathway of the Great Harvest. When people see the Jesus of the Word, the multitude will want to follow Him into His Kingdom. They will come. Many people in this generation have tried a little bit of everything; they can't connect with the "ho-hum" of religious Christianity, but the testament of His Glory, the proof of His reality, will attract them. Lord, You told me if I would lie before You I would see Your Glory; as Moses knew there was more to Your Glory than Your miracles, We know that Your glory is only released as You are able to reveal and magnify Your Son. Lord, Who You are was readily attested to by the witness of the supernatural. Your working of miracles revealed that You were indeed manifest as the Son of the Living God. Lord, we reach for the testament of Your Glory, the Son.

SCRIPTURE FOR MEDITATION:

"If I am not doing the works [performing the deeds] of My Father, then do not believe Me [do not adhere to Me and trust Me and rely on Me]. But if I do them, even though you do not believe Me or have faith in Me, [at least] believe the works and have faith in what I do, in order that you may know and understand [clearly] that the Father is in Me, and I am in the Father [One with Him]" (John 10:38-39 AMP).

WORD FOR THOUGHT:

Testament – *A witness; similarly testify, testimony, attest … tangible evidence; a tribute (Pey, 1977, p. 1016).*

MEDITATE ON:

All the particulars of all the great miracles that are testaments to His revealed Glory of Himself. Don't stop at scripture, but those you read about and the many testaments you have been privy to.

RELATIVE PRAYER:

Show me your glory.

JOURNAL
A Reflection of Your Thoughts

PERFECT LOVE CASTS OUT FEAR

I recognize in my life that the more I am in His Presence the less I allow any fear to rise. The more I am in Your Presence, the quicker I move to recognize and squash the temptation of fear. For in Your Presence is the sense of being covered and surrounded by Your Person. In this place of heart and mind, it is just you and I and I am so secure; a feeling that I believe I was deprived of for most of my life. In the Book of Ruth, Naomi tells Ruth, "My daughter, shall I not seek rest for thee, that it may be well with thee?" (Ruth 3:1). She tells her to go and lie at Boaz's feet and Ruth does just what Naomi says, and she asks Boaz to spread his skirt over his handmaid. He in turn tells her to fear not, that he would take responsibility for her well-being.

That is what our Lord does for us, as we take the time to lie at His feet and ask Him to cover us with His Person. "He brought me to the banqueting house, and His banner over me was love—for love waved as a protecting and comforting banner over my head when I was near Him" (SOS 2:4 AMP). There is no way you will not feel and know you are completely safe and covered, because you are in His Presence. We as Christians, filled with the Holy Spirit, are not in tune with His Presence in us or around us. I believe Christians are so much more aware of themselves (ministry, goals,

> *I recognize in my life that the more I am in His Presence the less I allow any fear to rise.*

people) than anything else. Oh Lord, I do remember the many times, especially in church, You had to shut me out in my thoughts so I would get in contact with Your Presence. We fall even short of Old Testament saints like Daniel who slept in the lions' den and didn't have the Holy Spirit within; even the New Testament saints like Peter, who knew he was to die after the Feast Days, but was still fast asleep when the angel woke him and told him to gird himself in preparation to leave the prison. "Am I a God at hand, saith the Lord, and not a God afar off?" (Jer. 23:23 KJV).

Surely Psalm 91 is coherent with the concept of His Presence where fear cannot reside.

> He who dwells in the secret place of the Most High shall remain stable and fixed under the shadow of the Almighty [Whose power no foe can withstand]. I will say of the Lord, He is my Refuge and my Fortress, my God, on Him I lean and rely, and in Him I (confidently) trust! For [then] He will deliver you from the snare of the fowler and from the deadly pestilence. [Then] He will cover you with His pinions, and under His wings shall you trust and find refuge; His truth and His faithfulness are a shield and a buckler. [Then] you shall not be afraid of the terror of the night, nor of the arrow [the evil plots and slanders of the wicked] that flies by day, nor of the pestilence that stalks in darkness, nor of the destruction and sudden death that surprise and lay waste at noonday … Because you have made the Lord your refuge, and the Most High your dwelling place, there shall no evil befall you, nor any plague or calamity come near your tent (Psalm 91:1-6, 9-10 AMP).

Being secure in His love will change our whole outlook on life, which may be hard for some, who have not known anything that corresponds to the God kind of love; but I admonish you to lie there with Him. He has a way of proving Himself to you.

SCRIPTURE FOR MEDITATION:

"There is no fear in love - dread does not exist; but full-grown (complete, perfect) love turns fear out of doors and expels every trace of terror! For fear brings with it the thought of punishment, and [so] he who is afraid has not reached the full maturity of love - is not yet grown into love's complete perfection" (1 John 4:18 AMP).

WORD FOR THOUGHT:

Rest *– to cease from action or motion: refrain from labor or exertion: to be free* *from anxiety or disturbance: to remain confident: to cause to be firmly fixed (Merriam-Webster).*

MEDITATE ON:

His promises of care and protection which let us rest in His word. Muse on His Words in Psalm 91 and realize you are in His Omnipresence. See yourself being overshadowed and covered by His awesome wings in the Holy of Holies, then envision the word that declares angels are in charge over you. You are too loved to be distressed.

RELATIVE PRAYER:

Lord, I know that all words have the power to relate pictures to our minds. Lord, let Your words in Psalm 91 relate just those visions that will cause us to see and know Your Truth.

JOURNAL
A Reflection of Your Thoughts

_____

_____

_____

_____

_____

_____

_____

_____

_____

_____

GOING FARTHER

T here are some places in God you will not know unless you determine to make yourself go farther. You must come to that place where your desire for God is persistent; you have no intention of letting up, for you must have more. You must come to this place of craving, where it is not about other people and what they are doing. This craving must become your pivot point. Many times saints look at others with the attitude, "I'm as good as the next," and fail to heed this craving or stirring which the Holy Spirit is initiating in our lives. This "I'm as good as the next" attitude can shut down or hinder the working of the Holy Spirit who knows the will of God for your life.

When I look at the scriptures, I see that the men and women who pleased God were those who were willing to go farther. Abraham was willing to go farther than his father, so much farther than even his heart and understanding could take him. When I look at Jochebed, she was willing to go farther than her fears to save her child. Ruth was willing and went farther than Orpah. You must realize we are not talking about ego here. We are talking about the Holy Spirit's unction in your life that is like a badgering voice in your spirit telling you to advance. He knows you are fearful, withdrawn, unworthy and like to stand in the shadow of others – like Moses, Gideon, Esther, Jeremiah, Mary, Timothy, etc. This calling seems to be out of the box, and you have only read about it in the Word or heard about it, but never actually seen it happening to you. Yes! It is for you, the unction to reach higher, go deeper and advance further.

I had a dream from the Lord that I was following this person. I never really saw Him, just a silhouette. At first everything was familiar, but then things got

31

dark and I was not sensing my way. Solomon says, "the Lord said that He would dwell in the thick darkness" (1 Kgs. 8:12 KJV). This was not the best feeling, although I sensed the supernatural happening. I knew the person was still in front of me although I did not see Him any longer. I was fearful, but I kept hearing His encouragement for me to keep coming. I sensed I was going higher, but it became so totally dark. Then suddenly I came upon the biggest glistening diamond I had ever seen and I felt the Lord's sweet love. I awoke with a complete understanding of God definitely telling me that no matter what it looks like, I must keep following Him. Keep going further in my quest for the things of God, because it would pay off. Many times things do not show up when we expect; we will limit the time we will wait before we go back to fishing (as the Apostles) and decide we had it all wrong, or could not have heard correctly. This is the time we must press beyond the breaking point of defeat and walk into breakthrough. Our heart must be convinced that the voice is the voice of the Great Shepherd.

> *We are talking about the Holy Spirit's unction in your life that is like a badgering voice in your spirit telling you to advance.*

"Then you will call upon Me, and you will come and pray to Me, and I will hear and heed you. Then you will seek Me, inquire for, and require Me [as a vital necessity] and find Me; when you search for Me with all your heart, I will be found by you, says the Lord, and I will release you from captivity and gather you from all the nations and all the places to which I have driven you, says the Lord, and I will bring you again to the place from which I caused you to be carried away captive" (Jer. 29:12-14 AMP).

"When you call on Me, when you come and pray to Me, I'll listen. When you come looking for Me, you'll find Me. Yes, when you get serious about finding Me and want it more than anything else, I'll make sure you won't be disappointed" (God's Decree, MSG).

SCRIPTURE FOR MEDITATION:

"Call to Me and I will answer you and show you great and mighty things, fenced in and hidden, which you do not know – do not distinguish and recognize, have knowledge of and understand" (Jeremiah 33:3 AMP).

WORD FOR THOUGHT:

Further – Going or extending beyond; additional … (Pey, 1977, p. 343).

Farther – at or to a greater distance or more advanced point; more completely.

MEDITATE ON:

God is the same today, yesterday and forever (Hebrews 13:8). Ponder on all the ones He allows to see into the Heavenly sphere and even Heaven itself. The angels and the secret things He revealed to His friends, Moses, David, Stephen, Paul, Anna, Mary, John, etc. What will He delight to show you about Himself and His power?

RELATIVE PRAYER:

Lord, I want to know You, see You, touch You, and feel You in the beauty of Your reality. Lord, I want to look until I see, reach until I touch, stretch until all areas in and around me feel You in my presence continually. I know it is possible to those who believe.

JOURNAL

A REFLECTION OF YOUR THOUGHTS

BEYOND THE VEIL

Beyond the Veil is a term synonymous with a deeper walk with God. It should be, for it relates to a face to face encounter with His Glory (Shekinah). Those who have had a glimpse "beyond the veil" are the most profoundly excited and expectant people you will ever meet. No ho-hum for them. No, do not give them mediocre Christianity; their hearts are filled with the anticipation of another Glory visitation. It does not matter how many times they find themselves on the floor in humble adoration, all they want is another manifestation of the Lord.

The Tabernacle is a revelation of Christ and His finished work residing in the Glory. It reveals your advancement into a deeper walk and reveals your consummation into the Glory. A deeper walk in depth, a deeper walk in holiness, a deeper insurgence of true light, and a deeper walk of love. Just a tiny glimpse of this Glory will cause you to steer away from the "little bit will do you" bunch. They are vacillators. They vacillate from the Outer Court, back to the world, from the world, back to the Outer Court. But those who have been allowed to experience "beyond the veil" refuse to be drawn back, but say as Paul says, "… let us go on to perfection …" (Hebrews 6:1). They are people who are pressing on to know Him intimately, the Completer, the Consummator, the Finisher, Who is none other than Jesus, the Christ.

There are two veils that must be torn from top to bottom. When I say top to bottom I am saying that God Himself will orchestrate the ripping of these veils, just as God chose Jesus' instrument of death and orchestrated the tearing of the veil of His flesh. The veil of the flesh is the first to be subdued in our lives. Most of us we are encouraged to and want to mortify our members as we desire a deeper walk in Christ. Know that God Himself recognizes your desire and has a plan to help you mortify your flesh. The second is our soulish veil, which takes much time to subdue; you will find it must be dealt with harshly again and again. To subdue the soul there must be much time with the Word, seeing the the light of the Holy Spirit reveal the Word. The Holy Spirit tutors our spirit, renewing our mind and strengthening and reinforcing our soul man; old things have passed away, and all things are quickened and become new because of the Holy Spirit. Know that the only help for the soul is its renewal. When the soul of man is

A deeper walk in depth, a deeper walk in holiness, a deeper insurgence of true light, and a deeper walk of love.

———

renewed it will bring or open new dimensions in prayer (Altar of Incense), which is the catalyst to intimacy with the Lover of your soul. For the born-again spirit is always willing to reunite intimately with its likeness, but its hindrance is the soul.

The Inner Court speaks of being privy to revelation you do not receive in the Outer Court. The Holy Spirit, the revealer of the things of God, is pleased to show you the things most sacred to the Lord. "He will honor and glorify Me, because He will take of (receive, draw upon) what is Mine and will reveal (declare, disclose, transmit) it to you" (John 16:14 AMP). The ripping of this veil will give you free access to His chambers. Know that the spirit is always willing to go beyond the veil, for this is the place of newfound nativity. An unregenerate soul will always resuscitate the flesh (carnal nature). Know that the born-again spirit is always willing to go beyond the veil.

SCRIPTURE FOR MEDITATION:

"Now, to the One Who can keep you from falling and set you without defect and full of joy in the Presence of His Sh'khinah- to God alone, our Deliverer, through Yeshua the Messiah, our Lord- be glory, majesty, power and authority before all time, now and forever" (Jude 24-25 CJB).

WORD FOR THOUGHT:

Ultimate *– Farthest ... extreme; last as in a series; coming at the end, as of a course of action or a process; coming as a final result; final and decisive; as an ultimate check to progress; forming a final claim or object; His ultimate goal or purpose ... the final point; the final result; the conclusion ... (Pey, 1977, p. 1071).*

MEDITATE ON:

Where is the finishing place for you? What is the finale? At the end, is your ultimate

35

goal to be clothed totally with the person of Christ, to be covered again in His Presence as Adam and Eve were? The Holy Spirit must be acknowledged as the only One who can usher us into our finale.

RELATIVE PRAYER:

Lord, how far is far enough? We pray with Ephesians 1:18: that the eyes of our understanding be flooded with light, that we will understand the hope that we are called to, so to know the richness of our glorious inheritance. Holy Spirit, You are the Potter, and we will be Your clay.

JOURNAL
A REFLECTION OF YOUR THOUGHTS

_____

_____

_____

_____

_____

_____

_____

_____

_____

_____

_____

_____

RELATIVE READING - "RELATIONSHIP"

What would you say of your relationship with the Lord? No, I am not asking if you are saved; I am not asking about your confession of faith, baptism (Holy Spirit or water), nor am I asking how often you attend church. This question is not about what auxiliaries you manage, or how much you give to the missions and the church. These of course are good works and the works of righteousness. Do not let me or anyone else tell you that God does not expect these from you. "And Jesus answering said unto him, Suffer it to be so now: for thus it becometh us to fulfill all righteousness …" (Matt. 3:15 KJV). Our fellowship with Him is not just any fellowship, but divine fellowship. It is relationship with the Divine; something that we never deemed possible, not relating with man, but with His Divine Self. (I know I had no idea nor could I have imagined such a complete relationship.) When we have this divine fellowship with Him, we will do the things He did and would do now. Jesus said He only did what He saw the Father do and said what He heard the Father say. This is a relationship of Divine fellowship (His Goodness- Supreme Good) in the highest order. He says to us, "Behold, I stand at the door, and knock: if any man hear my voice, and open the door, I will come in to him, and will sup with him, and he with Me" (Rev. 3:21 KJV). "Look at Me. I stand at the door. I knock. If you hear Me call and open the door. I'll come right in and sit down to supper with you" (MSG). The word sup is defined as a time of supper or dinner (feast). This represents a time to partake. What will we partake? Jesus (Yeshua) will partake of us and we will partake of Him. Relationship comes when we hear His call to come and dine and we answer with delight and joy that the Master is calling us into fellowship, intimate "koinonia." There is an old song that uses these words, "I come to the garden alone; while the dew is still on the roses." Yes! He will spend this type of time with you. He knows everything about you, your fears, shyness, feeling of rejection, desires and hopes. Rest assured He is the only One who knows you completely. Our relationship leads us to want to know His heart; we will find that His heart is gigantic; His heart accommodates things we couldn't fathom, surely He knows us all. Relationship comes through spending time with Him, a desperate need to feel Him, touch Him, see His face. People can tell you a lot of things, but you will never know Him until you seek Him with all your heart. Then the Lord says He will be found of you (Jer. 29:13). "When you come looking for Me, you'll find Me" (MSG). "Then you will seek Me, inquire for, and require Me [as a vital necessity] and find Me; when you search for Me with all your heart" (AMP). There are some things that seem to be basic for those Generals of the Faith who have or have had a tangible relationship with the Lord. So I have gleaned and learned from their experience, which is also now my experience: seeking Him with our whole heart takes time, and the elimination of things that hinder closer relationship with our Lord, even harmless things that hinder and distract. "Take us the foxes, the little foxes, that spoil the vines: for our vines have tender grapes"(SOS 2:15 KJV). "Catch the foxes, the little foxes, before they ruin our vineyard in bloom" (GNB). Pastoral Poetry says, the fox is a "thieving fox;" he comes to steal what is rightly yours. Relationship is our right, because of the Blood of Jesus (Yeshua) that washed and purified us. If you can help it do not allow space and distance to come between your personal fellowship with Him. Be consistent. Your capacity for praise and especially worship is an indicator of your relationship with Him. Praise and worship should never only be experienced in the corporate setting of the church. The Holy Spirit is the Matchmaker in our relationship, so when you sense His drawing, no matter what you are doing, follow Him into special time alone with your Lord. When the Holy Spirit is bidding us into time alone and away with Him, if we will follow, there is a special blessing for us. The prince of the air has duped this generation with many distractions, all related to the airwaves: telephone, television, internet. Quantity is also a must; fifteen minutes is good, but one hour is better; one hour is good, but two hours is better. Eventually the time to spend will be made explicit by your acquired desire. The Lord sent a representation of Himself to me in a dream and He was singing to me that He wanted me to feel His heart. I knew He was asking me for more time. Just know that He is passionate about us and that we are part of His heartbeat. If we do not ignore the Holy Spirit, He expresses His desire quite well. The final thing I would suggest is to read books and articles from the Generals who had amazing knowledge and relationships with the Lord. God wants us to be in full awareness of Him in our daily lives; He is with us (Emmanuel). Neglecting this is a huge loss to any born-again Christian. We have not trained ourselves to awareness of the One who indwells our Temple (body) at all times. There is reason to "Practice His Presence." I started talking to the Lord all the time, because I was always so needy. I eventually came across *The Practice of the Presence of God*, by Brother Lawrence, and I began to locate my relationship with the Lord. God has been there for us throughout our lives, but we were not aware of Him. We can't just acknowledge Him; we must begin to truly relate in a personal way. When you wake in the morning do you see your wife or husband face to face and not talk to them? He has always been there for us, but like me most of us do not relate to communing with Him as we do with a natural human being. Jesus talked to the Father constantly. I heard a true story from a man as he was searching for his true

Your capacity for praise and especially worship is an indicator of your relationship with Him.

mate. He looked from state to state, from one conference to another. One day while at his local church he said he heard a voice tell him that a certain young lady was his true mate. He had never considered this young lady, but from that time on he began to be aware of her. There were many things he liked. She had always been aware of him and knew she would like to marry him. To shorten the story, they did get married and he explains as time went by her worth and value multiplied increasingly; he realized what a prize he had, and he began to treasure what was there all the time. He was looking everywhere else, but was not aware of what was right there for him. I give this true story, because we are like this young man, seeking everywhere else for an intimate relationship, and Jesus has been there all the time. Conference times are nice, but He awaits our time just with Him. So many enjoy fellowship with the saints, but have not learned to really fellowship with the Lord. The fellowship, communion, partnership, "koinonia" rearranges our mind in every way. There we will positively learn His greater value in our lives. Relationships are sustained through commitment, honor, truth, and faithfulness. Love is the seal. Relationship is the master key (fits every lock) to the greater things of God. I have found we can relate our positioning and progress in Christ by looking at our process as found in the Tabernacle; for the tabernacle is Christ and it will indeed show our procession in His life. When we first come to Christ we find ourselves in the place of acceptance, no matter the mess we are coming from we are accepted into the beloved. This place refers to the outer courts where we carry the baggage and burden of many excesses, things that are detrimental to us. The Brazen Altar and the Brazen Laver meet us in the Outer Court to alleviate us from these burdens. This place of Blood and washing is sufficient to handle all our sins and maladies that will hinder relationship with our God. Then we are to seek to advance our relationship. The Holy Spirit woos us into greater communion with Him. "Then shall we know, if we follow on to know the Lord: His going forth is prepared as the morning; and He shall come unto us as the rain, as the latter and former rain unto the earth" (Hosea 6:3 KJV). When we follow on, pursue and become attentive to this new life in Christ, "We're ready to study God, eager for God-knowledge. As sure as dawn breaks, so sure is His daily arrival. He comes as rain comes, as spring rain refreshing the ground" (MSG). "Yes, let us know - recognize, be acquainted with, and understand Him: let us be zealous to know the Lord (to appreciate, give heed to and cherish Him) His going forth is prepared and certain as the dawn, and He will come to us as the [heavy] rain, as the latter rain that waters the earth" (AMP). As surely as a newborn desires the breast you will desire the sincere milk of the word. God requires us to search the scriptures, for in them you find life and your new birth experience. This place is the Inner Court, the place of courtship. You will learn of Him and receive the needed knowledge to fall deeply in love with Him. Sometimes we think we really love Him in the outer court, but the inner court is the place to fall deeply in love with Him. The Holy Spirit is the floodlight that reveals our Savior and how beholden we are to Him. We love Him, because He first loved us. There is no other light in this place, no natural light, all knowledge and revelation are made known by the Holy Spirit Himself. That is why we can never expect people in the world to understand what we are privy to and know with certainty. The Table of Shewbread (face/presence) is the Word of God, the true manna from heaven. As we began to know Him, learn of Him and His will is made known to us, our prayer offering will become golden, divinely orchestrated. These are prayers after His will, to His delight, which could be offered only with the revealed knowledge accommodated by the Holy Spirit. As I said, this is the place of courtship, loving Him, enjoying Him and giving Him your time. He is loving you and enjoying you, revealing Himself to you. It is from this place that the Holy Spirit will be obliged to call you into the Holy of Holies; the Holiest place of all. For some people the word holy or holiness is considered taboo; many are afraid they will turn the masses away if they talk of His holiness. If we are to have relationship it can only be with a Holy God. This is the place of Oneness, the place of consummation. This is the place where you can live through the spirit by the Spirit. This is the place where you live in and out of your High Priest Jesus (Yeshua). Remember that only the High Priest could go into the Holy of Holies; now we may go into this holy place, but only in Christ. This is the place where we are assured heavenly attendance, where we abide in His fullness and He abides in us tangibly, and therefore we can ask what we will and it will be given to us. We want to ask what we will, but are we abiding in this place? God will answer His people when they call; know the confidence in abiding. This is what I believe is right relationship with the One with Whom we have to do. Your whole you have submitted to Him. Remember Jesus (Yeshua) said, "I know You hear Me always, because I do those things that please You." This is the place where the flesh has been dealt with in the Outer Court; the Holy Spirit transformed and regenerated the soul man in the Inner Court. The Holy of Holies is for spirit to Spirit communion. Your spirit has been tutored by the Holy Spirit and once again can abide in "Shekinah" Presence. Please be advised that it is Spirit to spirit. This is the only combination that will truly mix and retain its consistency. Just as water and milk or oil might seem as though it has mixed, just give it a while and you will know it really has not. Water and water can truly mix and remain in that state and cannot be separated, so Spirit and spirit can mix (consummate) become One to the Glory of the Father, bringing forth much fruit. This is the relationship the Lord desires with us. Remember, you can thank and praise Him without relationship, but worship is key to relationship; relationship brings Presence and Presence releases the tangible Glory (Shekinah).

WEEK THIRTEEN

I CLING

I cling to you, Lord, like wet to water. I don't want to ever drop my grip and I ask You to never lose Your grip on me. I know I have not always given You a reason to hold on to me and I am truly sorry, but I am so glad my mistakes did not detour Your Love and desire to have me for Your own. Your hand that holds me, Your arms that embrace me, have proven to be firm and strong. Amidst all the tumult that has tried to emotionally and mentally confuse me, and the commotion meant to keep my life full of agitation; I still desired to cling to you. These were attempts to nullify my closeness and place in You. My response was to hide and be covered with Your Feathers, to trust under Your tenacious wings. I remember the times when I first began to walk with You, I would feel frustrated and like I was not keeping the same desire I had at the beginning. That was such a scary thought. I would cry out frantically and beg You, "Please don't even let me ever consider leaving You," because I knew I had what my soul longed for. I didn't want to imagine going back on You.

> *Lord, I do realize even though I call myself clinging to You, it was not my power or strength that kept me, but Your clinging to me that has kept me.*

Lord, I do realize even though I call myself clinging to You, it was not my power or strength that kept me, but Your clinging to me that has kept me. The scripture declares, "Who shall separate us from the love of Christ?" (Romans 8:35 KJV). It is not my love for You that is so strong, settled and powerful; certainly it is Your Love for me that makes this statement true. Sometimes I

41

feel I am holding on for dear life, yet knowing you have me. There is a song I just perfectly love: "Your love never fails, it never gives up, it never runs out on me ... On and on and on and on it goes, for it overwhelms and satisfies my soul" ("Your Love Never Fails," Chris McCartney).

This I have experienced and must acknowledge; my vain thoughts of clinging to You can be considered honorable attempts, but the bottom line is, and I admit, it is all about Your Love that clings to every part of my being with tenacity and retentiveness. There is no greater delight than my feelings of Your possessiveness for me. I can never belong to another. You and You alone can secure what I experience and feel in Your Presence. I cling. I cling, Lord with all my being. No closeness I would rather have than Yours. Cling Lord. Cling to me.

SCRIPTURE FOR MEDITATION:

"And may you love the Lord your God, obey His voice, and cling to Him. For He is your life and the length of your days ..." (Deuteronomy 30:20 AMP).

"And love God, your God, listening obediently to Him, firmly embracing Him. Oh yes, He is life itself, a long life ..." (MSG).

WORD FOR THOUGHT:

Tenacity – *The quality or property of being tenacious; firmness in holding fast; retentiveness; persistence or obstinacy; adhesiveness; cohesiveness; toughness ... (Pey, 1977, p. 1012).*

MEDITATE ON:

God wants you! We don't and can't so easily get out of His hands. Think on Him as a cohesive and adhesive magnet. He draws us to Him and He is the substance (Love) that's used to cause us to adhere solely to Him.

RELATIVE PRAYER:

Lord, the Bible says Ruth cleaved (clung) to Naomi and made vows to never leave her (and kept the vows), Lord, I do so ask you to help me keep my vows to cling to You forever.

JOURNAL

A Reflection of Your Thoughts

EXTRAORDINARY WEALTH

O h Lord, last night in the morning hours I was embraced by Your arms. When I awoke, I was filled with this enormous feeling of wealth, extraordinary wealth. This feeling is truly exceptional, I believe, to any other wealth. Lord, the time I heard Your intriguing, audible voice and the many times I heard Your inner voice, are the times I recognize my extraordinary wealth in You. The dreams and visions You have given to me equate to Your personal attentiveness in my life. Like the time I saw myself trying on all these very beautiful and exquisite gowns. They were purple, gold and silver. Then I realized someone was coming to look us over. (There were other people there.)

He came in and I never saw facial features, but the consensus was He was to be desired above all. He came in and then left. I didn't feel He had chosen me, but when the word came, I was indeed chosen. I began to go in to Him and this older woman stopped me and told me to come back, and she scolded me (in a way) and told me that I was not walking like a queen. I knew she was right because of how I was walking (walking with my head down, feeling unworthy), and I adjusted my mannerism and went in. I remember waking again to this most wealthy feeling. I don't remember if I had any money or accomplished anything that day, but Your speaking to me in this dream was the determining factor for me to feel so extraordinarily wealthy.

I have been blessed with things that I truly value. I have never yet experienced great monetary wealth. In Deuteronomy 8:18, God says that He will give us the power to get wealth and I truly believe this, especially today. This is talking about monetary wealth. We all need some of this and I want this blessing. Lord, You bless us in oh so many ways which have the capacity to make rich and add no sorrow to us (Prov. 10:22). The wealth to be had from intermingling with You is extraordinary in every facet. The wealth that will emanate from Your Person is a revelation of Your Wisdom, Your Power, and Your discernment, Your Love, and on and on and on it goes. Nothing else will ever compare to the feeling of this wealth. This passage in Jeremiah alludes to the comparison of knowing Him in all His love: God's message: "Don't let the wise brag of their wisdom. Don't let heroes brag of their exploits. Don't let the rich brag of their riches. If you brag, brag of this and this only: That you understand and know Me. I Am God, and I act in loyal love. I do what's right and set things right and fair, and delight in those who do the same things. These are my trademarks" (Jer. 9:23-24 MSG). The fact that I belong to You, You chose me when I was yet in my sins and washed me and perfumed me just for You, to be Yours for eternity is the wealth I choose to brag on.

> *The fact that I belong to You, You chose me when I was yet in my sins and washed me and perfumed me just for You, to be Yours for eternity is the wealth I choose to brag on.*

I really don't think anything compares to this. To be able to discern and acknowledge this wealth can only come through the Holy Spirit teaching us how to value You in a more perfect way.

SCRIPTURE FOR MEDITATION:

"But where shall Wisdom be found? And where is the place of understanding? Man knows not the price of it; neither is it found in the land of the living. The deep says, [Wisdom] is not in me, and the sea says, It is not with me. It cannot be gotten for gold, neither shall silver be weighed for the price of it. It cannot be valued in [terms of] the gold of Ophir, in the precious onyx or beryl, or the sapphire. Gold and glass cannot equal [Wisdom], nor can it be exchanged for jewels or vessels of fine gold. No mention shall be made of coral or of crystal; for the possession of Wisdom is even above rubies or pearls. The topaz of Ethiopia cannot compare with it, nor can it be valued in pure gold. From where then does Wisdom come? And where is the place of understanding? It is hid from the eyes of all living, and knowledge of it is withheld from the birds of the heavens. Abaddon (the place of destruction) and Death say, We have [only] heard the report of it with our ears. God understands the way [to Wisdom] and He knows the place of it [Wisdom is with God alone]" (Job 28:12-23 AMP).

WORD FOR THOUGHT:

Compare – to look at (two or more things) closely in order to see what is similar or different about them or in order to decide which one is better ... (Merriam-Webster).

MEDITATE ON:

The wealth you are aware of and can acknowledge now. Then begin to meditate on the truth that says, "eyes haven't seen and ears haven't heard and it hasn't even entered in our hearts the things that God has prepared for them that love Him" (1 Corinthians 2:9). That's why we have this scripture text: "No one's ever seen or heard anything like this, Never so much as imagined anything quite like it — What God has arranged for those who love Him. But you've seen and heard it because God by His Spirit has brought it all out into the open before you" (MSG).

RELATIVE PRAYER:

Lord, the riches of my inheritance are revealed through my constant desirous relationship with You. Lord, evermore, think on me often to give me this abundant wealth found in Oneness with You.

JOURNAL

A REFLECTION OF YOUR THOUGHTS

Don't allow your journaling to become a one night stand. These memoirs of Presence took many hours of enjoying and thinking of Him. Remember to take precious, devoted time for your journaling.

_____

_____

_____

_____

_____

_____

_____

WEEK FIFTEEN

THROUGH IT ALL

Suffering is not a pleasure, but in all our lives (in Christ) we will experience the suffering of the cross of Christ. That is why He tells us to take up our cross and follow Him. There are times when following Christ will bring suffering, whether it's rejection, gossip, loss, evil, trouble, or abuse: these are all causes of suffering. We don't know how to embrace these times; they always seem to be foreign or a hindrance to what we believe we should be experiencing in Christ. Our times of suffering are always under the watchful eye of our God; He neither sleeps nor slumbers. Many of these times that He didn't cause, He refashions to assure that they will work for our good for His glory. When these times of suffering come to us, we let the Lord know with strong resistance, "I'd rather not!" We see in the Song of Songs the Shulammite's resistance from her place of rest and comfort to come away into suffering with her lover. Let's look at this passage of scripture,

> "I am come into my garden, my sister, my spouse; I have gathered my
> myrrh with my spice; I have eaten my honeycomb with my honey; I
> have drunk my wine with my milk: eat, O friends; drink abundantly,
> O beloved. I sleep, but my heart waketh: [mystic sleep] it is the voice
> of my beloved that knocketh, saying, open to me, my sister, my love,
> my dove, my undefiled: For my head is filled with dew, and my locks
> with drops of the night. I have put off my coat; how shall I put it on?
> I have washed my feet; how shall I defile them? My beloved put in
> His hand by the hole of the door, and my bowels were moved for
> Him. I rose up to open to my beloved; and my hands dropped with

47

myrrh, and my fingers with sweet smelling myrrh, upon the handles of the lock. I opened to my beloved; but my beloved had withdrawn himself, and was gone: my soul failed when he spake: I sought him, but I could not find him; I called him, but he gave me no answer (SOS 5:1-6 KJV).

Myrrh is associated with suffering, bitterness and heaviness. The bridegroom's hands were dripping myrrh with the sweet fragrant smell that comes from the benefits of suffering (passion). God will call us into His suffering, which allots great glory to rest over us, just waiting to overtake us in due time. Paul said, "that I may know Him, and the power of His resurrection, and the fellowship of His sufferings, being made conformable unto His death" (Phil. 3:10 KJV). "Know" is a very strong word as it relates to intimacy. Him in me, me in Him, possessing one another, I can believe that He is never closer and more attentive than during the time He allows us to be One with Him in His suffering. It is possible that suffering introduces to us our greatest time for consummation (seeing, perceiving, discovery, familiarity, recognizing, learning, Oneness, finishing, completing, perfecting, becoming privy to His person). Because of my times of suffering I have a surety and respect that I never could have obtained from Him any other way. Many say there should be no suffering whatever for the Christian; but this doctrine is not in scripture. The good news is that we overcome and prevail to our God-given glory (2 Cor. 1:4-7). Andrae Crouch's song, "Through It All," comes to my mind. Here are a few lines of the song: "I thank Him for the mountains, and I thank Him for the valleys, and I thank Him for the storms He brought me through, for if I'd never had a problem … I'd never know what faith in God could do." In a Christian's life there will always be a reason for what seems to be sure madness; remember fragrant perfumes and the oil from the olives come because of the crushing.

> *I can believe that He is never closer and more attentive than during the time He allows us to be One with Him in His suffering.*

SCRIPTURE FOR MEDITATION:

"But in so far as you are sharing Christ's sufferings, rejoice, so that when His glory (full of radiance and splendor) is revealed, you may also rejoice with triumph - exultantly" (1 Peter 4:13 AMP).

WORD FOR THOUGHT:

Suffering: *"Pathema:" something undergone, hardship or pain, an emotion or influ-*

ence – affection, affliction, motion, suffering – derivative of "Pathos:" suffering, a passion (espec. concupiscence) (Strong's Conc. (Gk), 3804, 3806).

MEDITATE ON:

This acronym God gave me for the word suffer: "stretching you for future eternal reign." Paul says, "For I reckon that the sufferings of the present time are not worthy to be compared with the glory which shall be revealed in us" (Romans 8:18 KJV).

RELATIVE PRAYER:

Lord, that we may so love you, that the pleasure of knowing you flows with lavish love and peaceful enjoyment, and may it supersede any present suffering as it did in Paul's life. My love, feelings, desire, and need are for you, no matter what must be signed with forever.

JOURNAL
A Reflection of Your Thoughts

EXTRA ORDINARILY EXTRAORDINARY

t is through You only that we see life as it truly is. You are the One I live in and live for. You are extra ordinarily extraordinary. Nothing is like You through eternity's end, if it would be such. There is nothing that exists or nothing that will ever exist that fits extra ordinarily extraordinary, but You. Lord, certain terms can only be beholden to You. Like the word awesome; You only are awesome, that word belongs to You. A person said to me, "You know, you're awesome." I remember Lord You told me to reject such a claim, for it was a blatant lie and I heard the Holy Spirit tell me to correct the person firmly in love. I forbade them, for there is nothing about me or any of us that should leave anyone awestruck unless they have attributed God's glorious ways to man. Lord You continually leave me awestruck. I humble myself and reverently praise You in all Your authority and great power. I am consumed with You and by You. I truly live for the experience of You. I remember the day You virtually enveloped me into You. I had never known or even thought this was a possible experience, but Oh! the wondrous ways and experiences You have for us. The experience settled the issue and embedded in me that You are my secret place, my hiding place, my strong tower, and refuge. Surely Psalm 91 came fully alive to me. I have experienced some heavenly highs in You; the places I have been allowed in because You are Who You are. It is through You only that we see life as it truly is. The natural has its place, but there is a spiritual that can make the natural supernatural, and Lord, You are in complete control of it all. Someone said that to walk in the third or fourth dimension will cause you to lose your mind. I believe to walk consistently in the third dimension is to understand His thought and ways better than what should be humanly possible, and You haven't lost your mind, but found the mind of Christ. Moses knew and saw that You are extraordinary and still knew

You only are awesome, that word belongs to You.

there was so much more. I know, Lord, You have not allowed me to walk in this dimension consistently, but thank You for the times You have allowed me to get a glimpse of that place. What a priceless place to gain; it is worth our whole lives. This place where You vouchsafe that You are extra ordinarily extraordinary.

SCRIPTURE FOR MEDITATION:

"O Lord God, Thou hast begun to show Thy servant Thy greatness, and Thy mighty hand; for what god is there in heaven or in the earth, that can do according to Thy works, and according to Thy might" (Deut. 3:24 KJV).

WORD FOR THOUGHT:

Extraordinarily: *In an extraordinary manner; in an uncommon degree; remarkably; exceedingly; eminently.*

MEDITATE ON:

His wondrous works in your life and others'. Can you think of anything that can arise in your life that His greatness, wisdom and might can't handle? Do you believe He is able to reach and stretch in every direction in your life to fulfill His desire for your life? The one thing you probably shouldn't do is to try to figure how He will do it; just see Him in all of His "Bigness" and allow yourself to be mesmerized by this truth.

RELATIVE PRAYER:

Lord, I not trying to be mystic for that doesn't please You. You know me though, and I do want to experience Your miracles, the working of awe. You are so much more than we have desired. Show Your glory, signs, and wonders that the church so greatly needs to show forth Your True Person. Yeshua.

JOURNAL
A REFLECTION OF YOUR THOUGHTS

_____

_____

_____

_____

_____

_____

_____

_____

_____

_____

_____

_____

_____

_____

_____

_____

_____

_____

_____

_____

_____

_____

DANCE WITH ME

You chose me to dance with You. In years back it was unthinkable for a girl to ask a male to dance with her, but the male would choose the female. It was my desire, but it was You that initiated, called me out to dance before and with You. When I feel this urge or unction; I know it's You asking me to dance with You. At first it was such a private personal matter, but it has broken through all tradition to a full confession that "my beloved is mine and I am His." When I dance before or with You it is my statement of real love, exclusive love, no intruders, just You and me.

You chose me undeserving, unworthy, unable to measure up to the honor, but indeed I accept. First there was an amount of shame; for what will others think? Will they think I'm a showoff? Will they think I'm out of place and that this should only be done at home? Will I be disturbing them? I know that they will think many things, yet when You call me to dance with You I will dance unashamed with the Lover of my soul. Whether behind closed doors or in a crowded room, who am I to refuse the King's

> *You chose me undeserving, unworthy, unable to measure up to the honor, but indeed I accept.*

advances, the King's desire? You are King of all kings; to dance in Your arms makes me feel loved and brand new. I have no doubt it's Your desire to dance with me; Your desire corresponds to my desire to feel Your Presence and closeness. I remember the dream you gave me that informed me that on my arrival to heaven, you would take time to dance all night with me. This delighted my soul and warmed my whole person. You always know how to bring pleasure to my life.

I don't need any theological insight into my dream, for if God told me He would, He will. I know that dancing is not just all pleasure, but it causes me to feel you rhythmically, synchronizing my heartbeat, following Your heart filled with Your love. In the Presence of the Lord dancing is admirable. My movement follows the excitement and emotion received from the Holy Spirit. "Let Isra'el rejoice in their Maker, let Tziyon's children take joy in their King. Let them praise His Name with dancing, make melody to Him with tambourine and lyre; for Adonai takes delight in His people, He crowns the humble with salvation" (Ps. 149:2-4 CJB). Lord, I find myself engaged, occupied, interlocked with my King of kings. Yeshua, "A smile of completeness."

SCRIPTURE FOR MEDITATION:

"Let them praise His name in dance; let them sing praises unto Him with timbrel and harp" (Psalm 149:3 KJV).

WORD FOR THOUGHT:

Rhythm: *A regular reoccurrence of a function or action, as the heart beats.*

Admirable*: Worthy of admiration, reverence, respect, or affection; most excellent.*

MEDITATE ON:

There are things that your heart seems to call for and need, although your mind or intellect seems to oppose them. I am of course a huge fan of Kathryn Kuhlman and watch her dance and flow to the rhythm of her heart. In these areas can we complement our heart and silence our intellect.

RELATIVE PRAYER:

Lord, we are so given to tradition, peers, political correctness in Christianity, our pride, self-protection and so much more. I don't advocate being out of order or unseemly, but I want to truly know You, hear You, and follow you into Your good pleasure.

JOURNAL
A REFLECTION OF YOUR THOUGHTS

YOU'RE MY JEWEL

Diamonds are a girl's best friend." The world has so many clichés that can obscurely cause us to self-destruct. Who could really make a statement like this? Even to repeat it is to insinuate that it could possibly be true. When we are born again, we are introduced to the most exquisite Jewel of all time, Jesus. He is by far the rarest, most attractive, intriguing, stunning, breath-taking and valuable of all things to be had. His rarities are to be sought after, for there is no other but He. He holds this place all by Himself. He tells us there is not another God, He knows not any, making Him a rarity that only exists with Him.

He is so attractive that we are forcibly and constantly being drawn into His chamber (dwelling place). He is magnificently charming. His actions and voice have the power to influence my reasoning in His favor. His attractiveness compels me with delight. It is not magic, it is just who He really is.

When we are born again, we are introduced to the most exquisite Jewel of all time, Jesus.

So many times when I am focused on You, I find myself stunningly stupefied with this expression: "Who are You, Lord?" Just as the disciples asked, "What kind of man is this?" (Matthew 8:27), I say to You, Lord, there is no way we will ever be able to comprehend what it means to be You; You are God. All I know now intrigues me. You really do shine like a bright morning star, but brighter. I know my interest will not fail to be aroused to seek you forever more.

To know You and then to know You are still so unexplained, so clandestine. There will always be the unsearchable and hidden things about You that are still even more breathtaking. I am so full of excitement over You that I don't want to take my eyes from You. I feel great need to always keep bringing my focus back to You. Many don't know that the more we dedicate and consume ourselves with Your Word the more You release glimpses of Your Person. Your profound worth tells me I don't want to miss what You are willing to show me of Yourself. You are my Jewel that I value with my life, truly with my life.

SCRIPTURE FOR MEDITATION:

"And He that sat was to look upon like a jasper and a sardine stone: and there was a rainbow round about the throne, in sight like unto an emerald" (Revelation 4:3 KJV).

WORD FOR THOUGHT:

Breath-taking—*Having a shock effect that checks breathing momentarily; causing extreme pleasure, awe, excitement; thrilling.*

MEDITATE ON:

This song has always touched my heart, "Lord, You are more precious than silver. Lord, You are more costly than gold. Lord, You are more beautiful than diamonds, and nothing I desire compares with You" (Unknown). Surely, Lord, nothing of any value can mount up to Your Worth.

RELATIVE PRAYER:

Lord, shine, dazzle me and blind me only to You. Let me wear You with the pride of always understanding in my own small way Who You are and how great a One I have in me.

JOURNAL
A REFLECTION OF YOUR THOUGHTS

DARK NIGHT

The "Dark Night" as I have heard of it, is a time when you look and feel and seek and can't find the One your soul longs after. I have been privy to this time. You're in a seemingly dormant or torrid place. You know where you have been, but are not sure at all about where you are. At first you're frantic to ascend from this place, but the time duration usually teaches you it's best to be still with all resoluteness. You believe (trust) that this might be the most unfounded place you have ever experienced in Him. He is in control of your life and you trust Him to do in this time what is necessary to draw you even closer and deeper in the tangible Presence of His Person. After you refute and bind all demonic activity, you resolve to seek Him more, even though it feels like He is a million miles away from you. There are so many questions we ask Him, a major one being, "Have I, or how have I offended You?" We all offend in some area now and then, but did I really offend You this time, because I find myself in this crushing place feeling destitute; where my wants and my need for a touch from You, to hear, to sense you tangibly, leave me feeling so abandoned and deprived. My knowledge of Your Word says I am not any of those things; it's just "a dark night of the soul." During a "dark night of the soul" I had this dream where I was in this place and many babies and small children were coming to me and I would take them and lift them up to someone who was above me. I couldn't see the face of the person, but I knew I wanted that Person's attention. So as I lifted the babes up I would try to get the man's hands to touch me when He took the child from me. This didn't work and I realized He was avoiding me. I got very discouraged and as I was leaving He came to the stairway, called out to me and said, "It won't be long now." I really believe this was the Lord telling me I would come out of this dark place soon. I felt that He was telling me to keep doing the work of the kingdom; it wouldn't be long before I would feel Him and experience the tangible again. "The dark night" is a silent place, where you don't seem to have the same connection with the heavenly and His Presence that you once had. (I said, "seem to have.") It's a place where your relationship is hampered, because you can't get to Him like you want to. Even with this you're amazed that your hope is not shattered. Just know that there is purpose in everything God takes us through or allows us to go through. The night is said to be a time between dusk and dawn when there is no sunlight. Many good things happen in the night; even our bodies are restored, regenerated at night while we sleep. We sleep and don't question whether the morning is coming, we know that morning will come again, it always has, for that is God's process of order. After all, it is not morning that is the beginning, but night is the start of something new in God (Gen. 1:5).

> *Just know that there is purpose in everything God takes us through or allows us to go through.*

SCRIPTURE FOR MEDITATION:

"And God called the light Day, and the darkness He called Night. And there was evening and there was morning, one day" (Genesis 1:5 AMP).

WORD FOR THOUGHT:

Resolute: *Having a fixed purpose; determined; steadfast; bold; firm.*

MEDITATE ON:

You're resolute that no matter what you feel or what is happening, you resolve to trust Him and you will remain fixed, firm in purpose, determined and steadfast, as bold as a lion in the things of God.

RELATIVE PRAYER:

Lord, Your word says, "Your anger endureth but a moment; in Your favour is life: weeping may endure for a night, but joy cometh in the morning. Lord, by Thy favour Thou has made my mountain to stand strong: Thou didst hide Thy face, and I was troubled. I cried to Thee, O Lord and unto the Lord I made supplication" (Psalm 30:5, 7, 8 KJV). Lord, I cry!

JOURNAL

A Reflection of Your Thoughts

Week Twenty

ON THE LORD'S SIDE

L ord, I am on Your side. I love Your side. I'll shout from the mountaintop that I am on Your side. On Your side is the only place of fullness of peace and joy. Your side truly carries my hope for tomorrow. I never could have known or understood what the impact of my tomorrow would be without having a God like You in my life. Draw a line in the sand and I will always choose Your side. You keep me secure and Your wings cover me and there is rest just knowing I'm on Your side. The voice of my bridegroom draws me closer than close. I know and feel Your closeness and experience wholeness found only in being really close. It's like a marriage: the two become one. Surely, Your side is the place of abundant life (zoe). My life has blossomed and flourished in this place, on Your side. Before coming to Your side, Lord, the only way I could have possibly defined contentment was with the help of a dictionary, but now I am able to define it from my heart, for my heart possesses it.

There are those who cross the line to return to their old life, but by now we should know that everything that glitters is not gold. Most things are just a bunch of hype with no future of true hope. There is a song that recording artist Eddie James performs called, "I AM." One stanza says, "I AM your future, so leave your past behind." I left my past on the other side of Jordan and I am fully drenched in Your Person, and the call and promises of this side. Your side, no matter what it looks like is where all Your thoughts of good toward us can be fulfilled. "For I know [My] … thoughts of peace, and not of evil, to give you an expected end" (Jer. 29:11 KJV). I know I am special because I was chosen for Your side. This means that I am written on the palm of Your hand. This means that as the mountains are around about Jerusalem, so is the Lord around about me. All these promises belong to me and there are more. It's like when we would choose sides for different teams, and you wished to be on a certain person's side. It didn't matter when you were chosen, you were just glad to be on their side because you believed you were on the best and winning side. Many times you were chosen because you could play well, or you were liked or popular, and sometimes you were the last one to be chosen. We know this is not the case with Our God for the scriptures tell us we were chosen before the foundation of the world. Lord, You foreknew us and You pre-ordained us; we don't have to worry about sitting on the bench. You give to us to will and do of Your good pleasure (Phil. 2:13). I heard someone say, "He doesn't choose the equipped, but He equips those He has chosen." Truly we learn that it is not about who we are or what we can do for the kingdom. It's all about Your great love for us that allows us to be part of Your kingdom. It is like Ruth, who surely knew she had no right to be on the winning side, but humbled herself for the favor shown to her. She was a Moabite who wasn't even allowed to come nigh the Holy things. God chose her and she became the great grandmother of King David, who was a king, prophet and priest in the holy things of the Lord.

Lord, I know your side is the best and winning side, and I am so glad You chose me. Moses asked the children of Israel once who was on the Lord's side. I declare and I confess, I make known to all I meet, "I am on the Lord's side."

> *I declare and I confess, I make known to all I meet, "I am on the Lord's side."*

SCRIPTURE FOR MEDITATION:

"But you are a chosen race, a royal priesthood, a dedicated nation, [God's] own purchased, special people, that you may set forth the wonderful deeds and display the virtues and perfections of Him Who called you out of darkness into His marvelous light" (1 Peter 2:9 AMP).

"But you are the ones chosen by God, chosen for the high calling of priestly work, chosen to be a holy people, God's instruments to do His work and speak out for Him, to tell others of the night-and-day difference He made for you — from nothing to something, from rejected to accepted." (MSG)

WORD FOR THOUGHT:

Chosen: *selected or marked for favor or special privilege (a chosen few), one who is the object of choice or of divine favor: an elect person (Merriam-Webster).*

MEDITATE ON:

The great privilege of serving the Lord and being on His side. A song by Andrae Crouch says, "I don't know why Jesus loves me; I don't know why He cared; I don't know why He sacrificed his life; Oh, but I'm glad. I'm glad he did" (Crouch, "I Don't Know Why," 1971). And I get to serve Him. Oh, so many have missed it, but, Precious Jesus, You have chosen me for Your side. Selah (pause and really think – meditate – on this divine privilege).

RELATIVE PRAYER:

Lord, Your word says you have chosen me. I did not choose you first, and because you did choose me, help me and direct me that I may bring forth fruitfulness to abide to your honor and glory. Lord, instruct me, and teach me in the way that I should go, Lord guide me with Your eyes (Psalm 32:8).

JOURNAL
A REFLECTION OF YOUR THOUGHTS

SO MUCH MORE OF YOU

Lord, I want so much more of You. More of Your touch, more of Your love, more of Your Presence and more of Your face. God, it seems that I have an insatiable desire for You. Lord, You did this to me, I could not have of done this to myself, I just couldn't have done this to myself. It sounds so paradoxical, because I find myself hugely satisfied, but I find that I am also always ready to receive more of You. I do think of a surety it is because You have put the necessary things in my life that would bring me to this place. I know that You know how to create a place in our lives that only You can fill, and some of our experiences are to create that place for Yourself. Did you make a place in my life that would require me fulfilling Your desire for me? I began to look at my life one day and realized that certain people are no longer in my life, so many things have changed and I don't have a desire for so many things any longer. I remember You speaking to me, telling me how You purposely emptied my life of many things because there was so much of You that You wanted me to have. Lord, I can believe the measure of our desire for You can actually reveal the place You have in Your heart for us. If it was not You desiring more of me I don't believe I would have ever come to know that the throne is a most powerful place. We must all go there. (He tells us to come boldly to the throne of grace where we will surely find help in our time of need.) But the greater unity is in Your chambers. (This is a place where you're not asking for anything, just enjoying His imposing Presence moving deeply upon you, permeating your person.)

"May He grant you out of the riches of His glory, to be strengthened and spiritually energized with power through His Spirit in your inner self, [indwelling your innermost being and personality]" (Eph. 3:16 AMP). "I pray that from the treasures of His glory He will empower you with inner strength by His Spirit" (CJB). As you contemplate and meditate there is full joy there, and at His right hand are pleasures (sweetness, delightfulness) forevermore, but know it is He Who must request the honor of your presence. For everything Lord, is for You, by You and to You.

There is satisfaction in many things, but nothing satisfies like You.

═══════

It amazes me that I have so much thirst and hunger for everything that concerns you. Everything else I seem to be able to take or leave (movies, shopping, restaurants, etc.). I enjoy these things at times, many things, but there is no necessity for them. There is satisfaction in many things, but nothing satisfies like You. I feel myself always trying to climb higher into the heavenly things that reveal You, or I could say, I'm trying to fall deeper into the depth of Your secret dwelling place; it is all relative. This place is where we advance higher and deeper in progression in search for Your Person. We find ourselves approaching the magnificence of Your Throne Room, a place of Your Presence. We don't stop there and still fall deeper into the depth of Who You are; it's all amazing. Surely as David wrote that You are his portion, these sentiments echo over and over again in my being. You are my portion, you are my portion, you are my portion, and it will echo over and over again in my search for more of You. This insatiable desire just won't quit, won't rest, like a deer that pants continually for the water-brook. My soul longs, my heart is stirred for more of You. You did this to me. This is relentless and untamable, and why not? For there is so much more of you to experience. Holy Spirit draw me. Do it again and again and I will continue to run after You, my portion, my life's desire.

SCRIPTURE FOR MEDITATION:

"O my dove, that art in the clefts of the rock, in the secret places of the stairs, let me see thy countenance, let me hear thy voice; for sweet is thy voice, and thy countenance is comely" (SOS 2:14 KJV).

WORD FOR THOUGHT:

Insatiable – *incapable of being satisfied or appeased (The Living Webster Dictionary). Unquenchable; can't be extinguished; unappeasable.*

MEDITATE ON:

What brings you joy, what makes you happy, what makes you feel whole, secure and complete? What excites you, what incites love unspeakable and what has overwhelmingly captured your heart? Jesus! (Yeshua) That's why you will always want more.

RELATIVE PRAYER:

Lord, whom do I have in heaven but You, and there is none in earth that I desire besides You. I ask You in humility (so desirously) for more of Thee.

JOURNAL
A REFLECTION OF YOUR THOUGHTS

WEEK TWENTY-TWO

HEAVENLY PLACES

The Presence is a conduit into mystical sleep. If you've never experienced this, it is like being here, but with the awareness of being there at the same time. When I say there, I am referring to the heavenly realm. You sense you are in another sphere or domain (heavenly in nature). I have actually seen in this time angelic wings passing in my senses. The Spirit made me know that when you enjoy and crave His Presence with sufficiency of heart you are allotted the privilege of glimpses of the heavenly. Since the natural realm is so dominant and invading we must know and acquaint ourselves with how to access His Presence. The Lord wants our love and affections, "If you then be risen with Christ, seek those things which are above, where Christ sitteth on the right hand of God. Set your affection on things above, not on things on the earth" (Col. 3:1-2 KJV). He wants us to feel Him and see into Him. Believe me, knowing Him in this way is walking in faith, faith to believe that as I respond to His love with my love and affection, He will respond with His love and reveal Himself to me. The revelations of spiritual happening won't lie dormant as they do in most Christians. Most Christians only relate to Him through religious practices, but He is a God who has no problem showing His emotions. Many times He tells us in our dreams or visions how much He loves and cares for us; it is a confirmation of His Word. I call this sleep mystical, because your consciousness of the natural becomes limited and the heavenly invades your consciousness. You find yourself in this realm or atmosphere that can only be heaven's, and if it is heaven's then the throne of God with all His glory is there in the vicinity. This is beauty and wonder revealed. Many of Maria Etter Woodworth's meetings were invaded by visions of the heavens. Many were saved, delivered and freed through their supernatural encounter with the heavenly realm during her meetings.

When we spend much time in prayer with God, there seems to be a supernatural faith unleashed that allows us to access the heavenly realm.

This is probably no different than Jacob's sleep at a place he called Bethel (House of God), and the experiences of the other men and women of God who have encountered the heavenly. Paul talks

> *The Spirit made me know that when you enjoy and crave His presence with sufficiency of heart you are allotted the privilege of glimpses of the heavenly.*

about his encounter in the heavenly, "I must go on boasting. Though there is nothing to be gained by it … years ago [I] was caught up to the third heaven - whether in the body or out of the body, I do not know, God knows. And I know that this man was caught into paradise - whether in the body or out of the body I do not know, God knows- and he heard things that cannot be told, which man may not utter" (2 Cor. 12:1-4 ESV). Paradise was unveiled to Paul and he didn't have to die to see it. I remember Paul saying in scripture that he spoke in tongues more than all the people. Also, we know he was a man of constant prayer, as we hear him say many times, "I cease not to pray for you." The passionate believer needs to live for Him, in Him, and through Him, abiding every day in His Presence. This I believe promotes and incites a personable relationship with Him in His heavenly places. Right now! I will say of this place: it reveals, it is amazing and wondrous and keeps you fully in expectation and fulfilling satisfaction.

SCRIPTURE FOR MEDITATION:

"And he came to a certain place and stayed there overnight, because the sun was set. Taking one of the stones of the place, he put it under his head and lay down there to sleep. And he dreamed that there was a ladder set up on the earth, and the top of it reached heaven; and the angels of God were ascending and descending on it!...And Jacob awoke from his sleep and he said, Surely the Lord is in this place and I didn't know it. He was afraid and said, how to be feared and reverenced is this place! This is none other than the House of God, and this is the gateway to heaven!" (Gen. 28:11-12; 16-17 AMPC).

WORD FOR THOUGHT:

Heavenly - *Of dwelling in heaven; celestial; Of the heavens; Divine; of more than earthly purity or beauty. Perhaps from the same as "oros" through the idea of elevation;*

the sky; by extension – heaven (as the abode of God); by implication happiness, power, eternity ... air, heaven(ly) (Strong's Gk. Conc. 3772).

MEDITATE ON:

Oh, Lord, you are bigger than life and your domain (heaven) is larger than we can conceive. I can't imagine the vastness of all you really are. I truly love beholding more of You and Your heavenlies.

RELATIVE PRAYER:

That the angels of God may ascend from earth to heaven and descend from heaven to earth through prayer portals. Jacob had an encounter with the Living God as he slept in mystical sleep; I believe in encounters as I enter mystical sleep. Do it for me, Lord.

JOURNAL
A Reflection of Your Thoughts

_____

_____

_____

_____

_____

_____

_____

_____

_____

_____

_____

Week Twenty-Three

FRESH OIL

I n His Presence is fresh oil. In Your Presence, Lord, we may all find a constant flow of oil flowing from Your Person. We must all desire fresh oil; we must never limit ourselves to what has been, but as we open ourselves to Your Presence daily that outpouring can continue. Lord, I Remember the five foolish virgins (Matt. 25:3) who were not allowed into Your eternal Presence because their oil had run out. I remember Moses was to tell the children of Israel to bring pure oil for the light, to assure the lamps would burn continually in the Tabernacle where Your Presence dwelled. As we spend quality time in His Presence, we are saturated, smeared, and rubbed with the scent of His fragrance; Our Lord is the potentate; that is, so potent that there is no way that being in His Presence won't affect your total person. I remember once when I had put on some perfume and was later making a drink for dinner. I guess my finger got into the drink, because the perfume was so potent that it made the drink taste like the perfume. As we dwell in His Presence we are saturated with the anointing and go out into our areas of ministry invested with power and His fragrance to drive sickness, disease, and poverty from our surroundings. We leave this place of Presence ready to do His bidding in this world as we take the Person of the Gospel into our environment. I can say that there are times you will feel the fatness of the fresh oil and what

New, vibrant, fresh oil is possible every day when primed every day, as we delight in His Presence through one of our most holy sacrifices, time.

you are possessing seems to be flowing with no effort on your part. You feel like you can run through troops and leap over walls with hind's feet. There have been many times when the atmosphere of glory has risen and I prepared to minister with the laying of hands. The flow of His oil began to pulsate from my hands and I knew God the Holy Spirit was ready to make a difference. Smith Wigglesworth is reported as saying, "If it is not happening I make it happen." I don't believe he was being arrogant, but knew what he was carrying. New, vibrant, fresh oil is possible every day when primed every day, as we delight in His Presence through one of our most holy sacrifices, time.

SCRIPTURE FOR MEDITATION:

"You prepare a table before me in the presence of my enemies. You anoint my head with oil; my (brimming) cup runs over" (Psalm 23:5 AMP).

"But my horn shalt thou exalt like the horn of an unicorn: I shall be anointed with fresh oil" (Psalm 92:10 KJV).

WORD FOR THOUGHT:

Fatness – *"Deshen:" Heb. the fat; fatness, i.e. (fig) abundance; spec. the fatty ashes of sacrifices – ashes, fatness. Prime root: be fat, to fatten, to anoint, to satisfy, rich, fertile (Strong's Conc. Heb. 1878, 1879, 1880).*

MEDITATE ON:

Oil being symbolic of the anointing. It is also used in times of celebration: "Thou lovest righteousness, and hatest wickedness: therefore, God, thy God, hath anointed thee with the oil of gladness above thy fellows" (Psalm 45:7 KJV). The anointing destroys the yoke, releasing us from sorrow and grief to times of refreshing, restoration, and gladness. Meditate on the great need for more oil (Isaiah 61:10; 10:27). More oil means many things, but especially more sacrificial time in His divine Presence.

RELATIVE PRAYER:

Lord, give me a praying spirit. Lord, give me a seeking spirit. Lord, give me a staying (waiting) spirit that desires a steady flow of Your fresh anointing oil.

JOURNAL
A Reflection of Your Thoughts

_____

_____

_____

_____

_____

_____

_____

_____

_____

_____

_____

_____

_____

_____

_____

_____

_____

_____

_____

_____

_____

_____

Week Twenty-Four

SWEETER THAN THE HONEYCOMB

Lord, Your Presence is sweetness and it makes glad the heart. It is like being in a candy store; the very atmosphere is charged with delightful sweetness. You sense it, you feel it, the Fragrance seems to penetrate your being; I have experienced children in a candy store, their spirits are full of life, their faces the sure picture of delight, and it's hard to settle them down. This is how I feel in Your Presence at times, for the sweetest place I've ever known is in Your Tangible Presence. "All thy garments smell of myrrh, and aloes, and cassia, out of the ivory palaces, whereby they have made thee glad" (Ps. 45:8 KJV). They say that certain scents can translate you to your mom's kitchen in your hometown. Certain scents can translate you into memories past and cause you to feel what you felt at that time. The fragrance of the Lord should be a recognizable happening as we gather, that translates us into the Holy of Holies (Presence) of the Lord. Moses was told from the Lord concerning the apothecary, to

> take the best spices: of liquid myrrh 500 shekels, of sweet-scented cinnamon half as much, 250 shekels, of fragrant calamus 250 shekels. And of cassia 500 shekels, in terms of the sanctuary shekel, and of olive oil a hin. And you shall make of these a holy anointing oil, a perfume compounded after the art of the perfumer; it shall be a sacred anointing oil. And you shall anoint the Tent of Meeting with it, and the Ark of the Testimony, And the (Showbread) table and all

its utensils, and the altar of incense, And the altar of Burnt Offering with all its utensils, and the laver (for cleansing) and its base … And say to the Israelites, This is a holy anointing oil (symbol of the Holy Spirit), sacred to Me alone throughout your generations. It shall not be poured upon a layman's body, nor shall you make any other like it in composition; it is holy and you shall hold it sacred (Ex. 30:23-28, 31-32 AMP).

Every spice represents the Person of our Lord. Nothing and no one else has the fragrance of the Lord. He indeed was the sweet smelling, medicinal and suffering Savior. I remember the time I was asking the Lord to heal a woman who had been told to come to our church to receive healing. That morning as the praise and worship was going forth it was so captivating. I thought I began to smell this beautiful fragrance of perfume. I looked around to see where it was coming from; no one was near me and I had not put any on, so I said to the Lord, "Is this You?" It began to get stronger and more vivid; everything was so fragrant that I was beginning to taste it very strongly; I realized it was the Lord

> *The sweetest place I've ever known is in Your Tangible Presence.*

and knew that He was answering me, that indeed He would heal this woman. Truly the woman, who had a lung condition, was totally healed; she fell down and then got up proclaiming her healing, because she could breathe normally again, even in the midst of her shouting. Sometimes men think this sweetness thing is only for women, but David (the mighty warrior) declares that God is sweeter than the honey from a honeycomb. This makes us know it is for all. The scripture tells us that Esther bathed for 6 months with oils and fragrances to go into the Presence of the King. No king compares to King Jesus. He is the better, the best, and the ultimate, and we should desire to bring Him our best. Lord, I want to bring You my best and I am inspired to bathe and soak in Your Presence in praise, worship, and the Word. He is the Word and many times the Word is characterized as being milk and honey. Is there anything more worth our time then bathing in the milk and honey of the Word? Spending time worshiping and soaking in the fragrant Word before our Lord we become the recipients of His sweetness and delighted with His fragrance.

SCRIPTURE FOR MEDITATION:

"I have come into my garden, my sister, my (promised) bride; I have gathered my myrrh with balsam and spice. From your sweet words I have gathered the richest perfumes and spices. I have eaten my honeycomb with my honey; I have drunk my wine with

my milk. Eat, O friends, feast on, O revelers of the palace; you can never make my lover disloyal to me. Drink, yes drink abundantly of love, O precious one, for now I know you are mine, irrevocably mine! With his confident words still thrilling her heart ..." (SOS 5:1 AMP).

WORD FOR THOUGHT:

Soaking – *"Ravah" a prime root, to slake the thirst (occasionally of other appetites): bathe, make drunk, fill, satiate, satisfy, soak, water (abundantly) (New Strong's Conc. Heb. 7301).*

MEDITATE ON:

How sweet His Words are to you; meditate with soft worship music and fill yourself with the sweetness of His person. Voice from your mouth and being, just how sweet He is to you. I am a fan of the beautiful soaking music from Christian artists like Grace Williams and Catherine Mullins.

RELATIVE PRAYER:

Lord, I want to stay sweet on You. Let the sweetness of your fragrance permeate my very being. Lord, bid me to stay in your Presence.

JOURNAL
A REFLECTION OF YOUR THOUGHTS

_____

_____

_____

_____

_____

_____

_____

_____

RELATIVE READING: "PRESENCE"

"Thou [God] wilt show [reveal] me the path of life: in Thy Presence is the fullness of joy; at Thy right hand there are pleasures for evermore" (Ps. 16:11 KJV). "You will show me the way of life, granting me the joy of Your Presence and the pleasures of living with You forever" (NLT). God desires to dwell among us; He has always showed us that He wants to dwell and live among His people. As we look at the Garden of Eden (Presence), Tabernacle (Presence), Ark (Presence), Temple (Presence), Yeshua (Presence), Holy Spirit (Presence), and today the Church (Presence). He makes a strong statement of His desire. God's Presence is everywhere at all times. He is Omnipresence we know, "Whither shall I go from Thy Spirit? Or whither shall I flee from Your Presence? If I ascend up into heaven, thou art there: if I make my bed in hell, behold, thou art there. If I take the wings of the morning, and dwell in the uttermost parts of the sea; even there shall Thy hand lead me, and Thy right hand shall hold Me" (Ps. 139:7-10 KJV). "Is there any place I can go to avoid Your Spirit? To be out of Your sight? If I climb to the sky, You're there! If I go underground, You're there! If I flew on morning's wings to the far western horizon, You'd find me in a minute - You're already there waiting!" (MSG). "Am I a God at hand, saith the Lord, and not a God afar off? Can any hide himself in secret places that I shall not see him? saith the Lord. Do not I fill heaven and earth? saith the Lord" (Jer. 23:23 KJV). "'Am I God only when near,' asks Adonai, 'and not when far away? Can anyone hide in a place so secret that I won't see him?' asks Adonai. Adonai says, 'Do I not fill heaven and earth?'" (CJB). God fills all space and time.

I see scripture relate to three types of Presence: Omnipresence (universal) He is everywhere at all times. Omni means "all." He is everywhere in the cosmos, and not only in the physical universe, but exceeding into realms beyond. God is in the future, in the past, and resides in our present. As scriptures relate, there is nowhere that God is not. We must know that everything in this whole universe is within Him; if it was outside Him it couldn't exist.

Then there is the corporate presence; this refers to God being in the midst of His people. He tells us in scripture, "For where two or three are gathered together in my name, there am I in the midst of them" (Matt. 18:20 KJV). "And when two or three of you are together because of Me, you can be sure that I'll be there" (MSG). I know that by knowing His name and gathering in His name we can legally demand and experience Him and His power. "I will set [you] on high because [you] have known My name" (Ps. 91:14 KJV). The Lord has always promised to keep His people in His Presence. When Moses sought the Lord about His Presence for the Israelites, God said, "My Presence shall go with you, and I will give you rest" (Ex. 33:14 AMP). Again He said unto them, "And I will set My Tabernacle among you: And My Soul shall not abhor you.

And I will walk among you, and will be your God, and you shall be my people" (Lev. 26:11, 12 KJV). "I will set My dwelling in and among you, and My Soul shall not despise or reject or separate itself from you. And I will walk in and with and among you and will be your God, and you shall be My people" (AMP). From the very beginning His desire is revealed: The Lord in the midst of His people, coming together to laud their God and King.

He called to Adam and Eve in the cool of the day (time of His Presence—koinonia) and said, "Adam where are you?" He was saying, "I come to fellowship, intermingle, converse with you." Adam and Eve were hiding, trying to cover up their undone condition. We must never pull the covers over our sin, for that is the thing that will forfeit our privilege to enjoy the Presence of the Lord. We must remain naked before the Lord, clothed in His Spirit and Truth (HIM). The scripture says if any man sin, we have a blessed Advocate with the Father. He is so quick to forgive our sins and restore us again, because He loves to be in our presence. It is a total understatement to say that in His Presence is where we belong. He, Our Lord, says He will not allow His Soul to hate or despise us. I can't tell you how many times I needed to hear Him say these Words. Paul said, "For in Him we live, and move, and have our being; as certain also of your own poets have said, for we are also His offspring" (Acts 17:28 KJV). "We live and move in Him, can't get away from Him! One of your poets said it well: 'We're the God-created'" (MSG). He is no joke, but the air we breathe. God's Presence is intensified when your happiness is founded and dependent on Him. When there is not one area in life that can do without Him we are kept continually involved in acknowledging Him. When we stand in constant awe of Him who lives inside us, we find it so much easier to walk circumspectly, because of our awareness of Him. (Sin can't live in His Presence.) We must enjoy spending time with Him as much as He enjoys spending time with us. This is a problem for many, because they seem to value so many things above the corporate and One on one, Face to face fellowship with God. There will never be any comparison of worth once you truly find the Place of Presence.

I'm talking about the secret place that David talks about in Psalm 91:1. This was a Place that David knew to be in the presence of those winged creatures that guarded His Presence (Ark of the Covenant). Cherubim are a rich source of mystery; in the book of Hebrews they are purposely not explained because of the detail involved. Their relationship to the Glory is profound. "Above the Ark were the Cherubim of Divine Glory, whose wings stretched out over the Ark's Cover, the Place of Atonement. But we cannot explain these things in detail now" (Heb. 9:5 NLT). "Above {the Ark} and overshadowing the Mercy Seat were the representations of the Cherubim [winged creatures which were the symbols] of Glory. We cannot now go into detail about these things" (AMP).

The Almighty and the Cherubim dwell on high, above, in the community of the heavenly. So, it seems logical that when we are really serious about living and dwelling in His Presence, we should take seriously Paul's advice, "If then you have been raised with Christ [to a new life, thus sharing His resurrection from the dead] aim at and seek the [rich, eternal treasures] that are above, where Christ is, seated at the right hand of God. And set your minds and keep them set on what is above - the higher things - not things that are on the earth" (Col. 3:1-2 AMP). Anyone who is a true seeker I believe has heard of *The Practice of the Presence of God* by Brother Lawrence. We see the children of Israel practicing the Presence of the Lord as they followed the cloud, which represented the Presence of the Lord.

> And so it was, when the cloud abode from even unto the morning, and that cloud was taken up in the morning, then they journeyed: whether it was by day or by night that the cloud was taken up, they journeyed. Or whether it were two days, or a month, or a year, that the cloud tarried upon the tabernacle, remaining thereon, the children of Israel abode in their tents, and journeyed not: but when it was taken up, they journeyed. At the commandment of the Lord they rested in the tents, and at the commandment of the Lord they journeyed: they kept the charge of the Lord, at the commandment of the Lord by the hand of Moses (Num. 9: 21-23 KJV).

This sounds like Moses and the Israelites had to be practicing the Lord's Presence (especially the leader). Before I ever read Brother Lawrence's book I decided that I really wanted to know His Presence, for I had seen His Presence on certain ones and I wanted this. Pastor Benny Hinn has been a mentor of mine for many years. Although I've met him in corporate settings I didn't know him personally. So I put everything on hold and I determined to wait on the awareness of His Presence in my life. (Truly, I knew by the Word and through the Holy Spirit He was in my life.) I knew I was seeking for His Presence that would present itself in a virtual way. "The desire to want, to experience, the need for His glorious Presence is an action influenced by the Holy Spirit. Designed to confer some blessing upon His follower, He first infuses a desire in the follower's heart for the particular blessing He Himself wants to give, in order that He may hear and grant the request" (author unknown). I believe this scripture bears the truth of this quote: "Delight thyself also in the Lord; and He shall give thee the desires of thine heart" (Ps. 37:4 KJV). "Lord, thou hast heard the desire of the humble; Thou wilt prepare their heart, Thou wilt cause Thine ear to hear" (Ps. 10:17). "[Not in your own strength] for it is God Who is all the while effectually at work in you - energizing and creating in you the power and desire - both to will and to work for His good pleasure and satisfaction and delight" (Phil. 2:13 AMP). "That energy is God's energy, an energy deep within you, God Himself willing and working at what will give Him the most pleasure" (MSG). Can I say, as I sought out His Presence I really didn't know what way God would minister His Presence, but I believed He would not deny me. (He is no respecter of persons.) I began by telling God, "I am so here, I am so needy and I desire so much more of You." It seemed like I had sought and prayed for hours in these terms, adding scripture that agreed with this promise. "Then shall ye call upon Me, and ye shall go and pray unto Me, and I will hearken unto you. And ye shall seek Me, and find Me, when ye shall search for Me with all your heart. And I will be found of you, saith the Lord" (Jer. 29:12-14 KJV). "When you call on Me, when you come and pray to Me, I'll listen, when you come looking for Me, you'll find Me. Yes, when you get serious about finding me and want it more than anything else, I'll make sure you won't be disappointed" (MSG). I really wanted to know some of what Paul, Brother Lawrence, Benny Hinn, and

Long for Him to the point that you actually recognize you're being greedy.

other great men and women knew about His Tangible Presence. I always knew that my relationship would not be exactly like Jesus' (Yeshua) or anyone else, for the Father Himself designs each of our relationship with Him according to His good pleasure. Still, I wanted to know how close I could get to Him. I prayed for hours and eventually the prayer from my mouth dissipated and silence began to penetrate my being. My spirit was still reaching, seeking, and consumed with a longing that wouldn't quit. My soul was longing for a touch of the actuality of Him. Again, I reiterate that I knew how to walk by faith and not by sight, but I also understood what an able God we serve, always wanting to reveal Himself in ways we don't know (Jer. 33:3). I continued without any audible words. Every other desire that would cause commotion in my heart I had silenced and held hostage to my craving for Him. I do love the words of St. Augustine and I find them true in my seeking His Tangible Presence, "Your affections are the steps, your will is the way. By loving you ascend, by neglecting, you descend, for the heart is not raised as the body is raised, for the body to be raised, it needs to change place; for the heart to be raised, it need only change its desire." Your closeness, nearness, will match your need and your desire for Him. Please know I am not referring to ministry or service of any kind; I am speaking about your craving for Him. The word desire can imply cravings, to covet greatly, to lust after, to be greedy, to long for, to delight after something that is delectable to you. For your personal attendance in this heavenly place before the Cherubim you must find yourself in this kind of heated desire. Long for Him to the point that you actually recognize you're being greedy; the Tangible Presence requires the strength of the word greedy. The Hebrew word for Presence is "Panen" which means, face of God, person, Shewbread, sight, dawning. The Greek word is "enopion;" in the face, appearance. These are a few words that seemed to penetrate my thoughts from the Greek and the Hebrew: "in the face," "to see from the front." Here is one I especially like: "nearness to gaze with wide open eyes as at something remarkable." When we desire His Presence, we desire to behold His face. As you remember, the Inner Court represents the place of knowing Him, the shewbread was there and the Holy Spirit (Lampstand), which is always revealing His Person to us. "He shall glorify me: for He shall receive of mine, and shall reveal it unto you" (John 16:14 KJV). "He will honor and glorify Me, because He will take of (receive, draw upon) what is Mine and will reveal (declare, disclose, transmit) it to you" (AMP). If we are to look on His face and see His Person it will be through the Holy Spirit. The Lord's Presence can vividly be in your life or you can live with only an idle mention; this is totally up to you. "That God is here both scripture and reason declare. It remains only for us to learn to realize this in conscious experience" (A.W. Tozer). I read somewhere that in the science of quantum physics you must concern yourself with and intently begin to look for the object, and it will appear. When I read this, I realized it correlated with scripture. "[He] calleth those things which be not as though they are" (Rom. 4:17 KJV). Does God hide Himself at times? Yes! But this is just for a season. Why does He hide Himself? I believe there can be reasons we know not of, but I do believe in these reasons: He wants to increase our desire; we don't really understand His desire for us, so He brings us to the height of our desire. This enables Him to receive a recompence of His great desire. There is a greater measure He desires from us, so He encourages and draws us through dreams and tokens of love that will open numerous places in the spiritual realm. Jesus told us not to cast our pearls before swine, and He will not allow the holy places to be treated as common. We are a fickle people and what we value today becomes common tomorrow, but everything in His attendance is in awe of Him. Wherever there is true awareness of His Presence there will be elevation and advancement in the Holy Spirit. Remember, He desires to reveal and show us His Person, which without question is incalculable. Knowing the Person of Christ increases your value to His kingdom. Moses knew he could do nothing without Him, so he told God, "If Your Presence does not go with me, I will not go." His Presence brings greater surrender and when you know and are aware that He's occupying your space and time you find you are easily and quickly motivated to follow His leading. You seem to sense a flowing with the Holy Spirit. We must desire to be in His Presence, ever so close to Him.

We are circling in on the times of the first century Apostle; I do believe that God's intention for this time is for double portions and through scripture He has saved the best for last. Just the shadow of Peter healed the sick, for he was full of the Lord Jesus (Yeshua). "And to know the love of Christ, which passeth knowledge, that you might be filled with all the fullness of God" (Eph. 3:19 KJV). "[That you may really come] to know - practically, through experience for yourselves - the love of Christ, which far surpasses mere knowledge (without experience); that you may be filled (through all your being) unto all the fullness of God - may have the richest measure of the Divine Presence, and become a body wholly filled and flooded with God Himself}!" (AMP). Jesus said, "The wind bloweth where it listeth, [delights] and thou hearest the sound thereof, but canst not tell whence it cometh, and whither it goeth: so is every one that is born of the Spirit" (John 3:8 KJV). The Holy Spirit is said to move wherever He delights, is pleased, and is determined (listeth). I know this is the time of Tangible Presence (visible manifestation of Glory). Tangible: capable of being touched or grasped; perceptible by touch; material; capable of being possessed or realized by the mind; real; actual; evident (*The Living Webster Enc. Dictionary*). The cloud was tangible, the burning bush tangible, the cloud that filled Solomon's Temple tangible, Glory on the Mount tangible. "The knowledge that God is present is blessed, but to feel His Presence is nothing less than sheer happiness" (Dr. Allen Fleece, *The Knowledge of The Holy*, A.W. Tozer). When we as a body become more desirous and involved with His Presence we will again see and experience the wonders of a Glorified Savior. I ponder the possibilities of this scripture: "Then went up Moses, and Aaron, Nadab, and Abihu, and seventy of the elders of Israel: And they saw the God Israel: and there was under His feet as it were a paved work of sapphire stone, and as it were the body of heaven in His clearness. And upon the nobles of the children of Israel He laid not His hand: also they saw God, and did eat and drink" (Ex. 24:9-10 KJV). God allowed mere men to see Him. In what way did they see him? Will He allow me to see Him? Maybe a better question for God is, "Can I handle this wondrous display of Your reality? Will I follow on to know You this way?" "So let us know and become personally acquainted with Him; let us press on to know and understand fully the [greatness of the] Lord [to honor, heed, and deeply cherish Him]. His appearing is prepared and is as certain as the dawn, And He will come to us [in salvation] like the [heavy] rain, like the spring rain watering the earth" (Hosea 6:3 AMP).

GLIMPSE

O Lord, the most attractive and overwhelming atmosphere I know is still, always and forever the place of the glory realm. This is the place where you shine brilliantly and we receive glimpses of Your glory. Where we get to relate to your "Ism" in a continual fresh way. Many years ago the elderly saints would recognize a need to enter into these "shut–ins" where all you allowed yourself to do was pray, praise, read and worship. There was virtually no communication with anyone but Jesus. You allowed the Holy Spirit to guide you through this time. You could always feel the worth of this time, whether a few days or a week. When you came out of the "shut-ins" even though your bodies were weakened, your spiritual man felt strong and enlarged. Your relationship with your Savior was heightened and magnified. Dear Lord, these times are so necessary and beneficial to our walk with you. We should still be shutting-in and shutting-out with our reading, prayer, praise and worship. It's a time to minister before Him in love and gratitude, with all our humble needs before Him and our dependence and trust in Him. When everything is shut out but Him, He will give you that glimpse of His Person and Glory; and nothing will be more important to you. The Lord admonishes us not to cast our pearls before swine and He surely won't do it. God must know that you're going to handle something this precious in an honorable way. It seems, Lord, this generation (for the most part) has lost their reverence and order before the holy things You allow us to enjoy. Many don't even believe that it is possible to receive a glimpse of Your Glory. I believe that it depends on the condition of the heart or possibly what You see in our heart. I believe also people are not taught to want more than salvation. Surely the most important thing for all of us is to be born again, but without revelatory teaching the people stay right at the gate. Paul says, "Therefore leaving the principles of the doctrine of Christ, let us go on unto perfection; not laying again the foundation of repentance from dead works, and of faith toward God. Of doctrine of baptisms, and of laying on of hands, and of resurrection of the dead, and of eternal judgment. And this we will do, if God permit" (Heb. 6:1-3 KJV). To remain in dead works probably suggests you have not caught a glimpse of His Person and don't desire one. A glimpse means a quick passing view or a fleeting glance, which will leave us always wanting more. He is so all that and more, that even though you want more you're overwhelmingly delighted and gratified with the marvelous glimpse that happened; you just know you must be glowing. There is nothing ordinary about Jesus. When He was on the ship with the disciples and the storm was raging and the sea was blustering, He simply

When everything is shut out but Him, He will give you that glimpse of His Person and Glory; and nothing will be more important to you.

spoke to all the commotion to be still and in peace, and it obeyed Him. The disciples asked the question, "What kind of man is this?" On another occasion the people declared that never has a man spoken like Him. Lord, You are so copious and so plenteous; a glimpse of Your Magnificence is purely awe-inspiring and mind-blowing. You, Lord, are the One who has excited us and encouraged us and told us that this is possible: "Seek me with your whole heart and I will be found of you." Thank You, Lord, for allowing Yourself to be found of us. This kind of encounter brings true rest with no striving, no worry, just the atmosphere that penetrates your being in all satisfaction. One writer wrote these lyrics, "Just to Behold You as My King," and still another song that Christians love to sing is, "You Are So Beautiful to Me." David said, "One thing have I desired of the Lord, that will I seek after; that I may dwell in the house of the Lord all the days of my life, to behold the beauty of the Lord, and to enquire in His temple" (Psalm 27:4 KJV). "One thing have I asked of the Lord, that will I seek, inquire for, and [insistently] require: that I may dwell in the house of the Lord [in His Presence] all the days of my life, to behold and gaze upon the beauty [the sweet attractiveness and the delightful loveliness] of the Lord and to meditate, consider, and inquire in His temple" (AMPC). I use the Amplified because after you get a glimpse of His beauty and Glory there is continual meditation and consideration that never leaves you. With each thought of that glimpse you are inundated with awe. I believe this is a miniature release of heaven that allows us to catch ongoing glimpses of His glory, and a reflection of His Person. This will penetrate to the core of your being and satiate every cell until you feel no need for anything but Him, although you enjoy all the other great things He gives us.

SCRIPTURE FOR MEDITATION:

"And ye said, behold, the Lord our God hath shown us His glory and His greatness, and we have heard His voice out of the midst of the fire: we have seen this day that God doth talk with man, and he liveth" (Deut. 5:24 KJV).

WORD FOR THOUGHT:

Distraction – *That which diverts your attention from a needful focus; to draw the sight, mind or attention to a different object or direction; to agitate by conflicting passion; to harass.*

MEDITATE ON:

What is the distraction that agitates, conflicts with, or harasses your passion for Christ? Is there a passion that is equal to Christ? Settle the issue; there is a place for many things in your life, but allow nothing to compare or take the place of His Preciousness. You must refute and chase away anything that tries to enter His place of rare precious-ness. His place is in the Tent of Meeting, or possibly it seems more like that cleft in the Rock. Enter this place often; this is where you can catch a glimpse of His glory.

RELATIVE PRAYER:

Lord, my heart, my heart, search it and if You find anything that holds You at bay, I must change it. I want to behold You. I am nothing compared to Moses, but he was receiving from the old covenant promises. We are to receive from the greatest covenant of promises every. Oh! How I want to see your glory.

JOURNAL
A Reflection of Your Thoughts

_____

_____

_____

_____

HOW DO I LOVE THEE

This day I began to ponder my life and why I love You so. Of course, scripture says, "We love Him, because He first loved us …" (1 John 4:19). Elizabeth Barrett Browning wrote, "How do I love thee? Let me count the ways." With You, God, this is an impossible task. I began to write down some of the ways and my heart began to swell with so many reasons; they began to surface so readily from my heart to my mind. It was not a mind thing, but it was a heart thing. We should know that it is out of the abundance of the heart that the mouth speaks. Lord, I started this task as a challenge to myself. Of course, Lord, You know I could never finish this task. Here are some of my reasons for loving You:

1. You chose to save me.
2. You loved me when I wasn't worth saving.
3. All my life I had known nothing but darkness and You translated me into Your kingdom.
4. You've saved my family, because Your Word is so true.
5. You're so loveable, rare, and precious.
6. I enjoy you.
7. You are so good (extraordinarily good).
8. You are a true treasure.
9. You make me feel special and valued.

10. I never knew true wholeness and completeness until you entered my life.
11. You are exactly what I always needed.
12. You are exactly what I always wanted.
13. You have proven to be my right one.
14. You are all Holy and I am in awe of You.
15. There is so much of you.
16. YOU

These are simply just the first things that surface. I am the beneficiary of love I never knew was possible until You. Why we love Him should be inexhaustible; the only exhaustible thing would be to run out of words to articulate this love. To meditate on Him opens a bottomless fountain of reasons we love Him as we do. Lord, the life I live has become all for the love of You.

> *Why we love Him should be inexhaustible.*

SCRIPTURE FOR MEDITATION:

"We love Him, because He first loved us" (1 John 4:19).

WORD FOR THOUGHT:

Inexhaustible – *impossible to deplete, empty out, exhaust in strength, might, wisdom, love, mercy, etc. … No one can hold this attribute but Him.*

MEDITATE ON:

Think on His love ever so often; never stop adoring Him for the profundity of His love. Any love you may have known will never be able to stand alongside His perfect love. For truly His love receives the seal as the only proven, perfect, amazing and overwhelming love to be had. His love has proven to be never failing and steadfast, even when we have reason to believe it should fail us (Lamentations 3:22-23).

RELATIVE PRAYER:

Lord, I want to know You in the fellowship of Your love; to know the love of Christ that passeth all knowledge; Lord I want to really come to know you practically through experience for myself (Ephesians 3:19 AMP). Lord help me to relate this unfeigned love to others.

JOURNAL
A Reflection of Your Thoughts

SONG FOR LIGHT

I n His Presence, in His Presence there is joy, wonderful joy; I will linger, I will stay in His Presence day by day; I will linger, I will stay in His Presence day by day; until His likeness will be seen in me." A God-chaser's heart will have an overflow of melody and song that's transmitted from within. At any time we are inspired by the Holy Spirit to sing a song to the Lord. Melody and song seem to really enlighten the heart. "In Him was life and the life was the light of men. And the light shineth in darkness: and the darkness comprehended it not" (John 1:4-5 KJV). Light dwells with Him; song and melody release an enhanced atmosphere of His Presence. The Light of His Presence abolishes all darkness, and He inhabits the song of our praise. This is the closest we will get now to live in a world without darkness. His Word is a light to our path and a lamp to our feet. David the great psalmist was a man who knew and understood the value of putting melody to the Word of God. His words of praise brought light to the darkness. Every word of the Holy Writ can become a song light. According to scripture the Word is light and when you put song to the Word you are much more likely to retain the light of that Word. Also know that every word of praise coming out of your heart can most likely be translated into a song of praise that will enlighten someone. A song has the privilege of giving light and hope in dark places. A melody has a way of freeing your mind. God can speak to us in many ways and one of them is through song. I remember when the Lord told me to return from my hometown back to California; I did not want to do that. I was obedient, because I had received numerous confirmations, so I packed up and sent everything toward California and the next morning I was to leave. I went to sleep that night, but I still had a heavy heart. That night there was a song that I heard literally all night in my sub-consciousness. I woke up and realized it was a song that I hadn't heard for a very long time, "I Will Go with You All the Way." This song didn't let up all night and I realized this was the Holy Spirit assuring me that He was with me. He had brought light into my situation through a song. Many times we begin to sing a song for what seems to be no reason, but listen to it, think about it. Could it be a source of light you need for that time? Do the words find a place in the now? Thank You Holy Spirit.

According to scripture the Word is light and when you put song to the Word you are much more likely to retain the light of that Word.

To make melody in your heart for Him carries with it many times the grand reward of light, illumination and clarity. We can't focus on the things of this world. We must be careful that we don't sing the "woe" songs that entertain darkness unaware, having the power to bring darkness into our presence. "But no one asks, where is God my Maker, Who causes glad songs to ring out at night" (Job 35:10 CJB). So sing unto the Lord, sing unto the Lord a new song. Make melody in your heart and fill your environment with His light that drives the darkness at bay.

SCRIPTURE FOR MEDITATION:

"Wherefore be ye not unwise, but understanding what the will of the Lord is. And be not drunk with wine, wherein is excess; but be filled with the Spirit; Speaking to yourselves in Psalms and hymns and spiritual songs, singing and making melody in your heart to the Lord" (Ephesians 5:17–19 KJV).

WORD FOR THOUGHT:

Melody – *A sweet or agreeable succession or arrangement of sounds; a poem composed for singing to some melody or tune (Webster's Dict.).*

MEDITATE ON:

The songs you've sung today or this week have come from a release of your spirit. Songs that seem repetitious or new songs can come also as a message from the Holy Spirit. He lets us know many times that He is aware of our thoughts and needs by what songs the Spirit releases. I remember the little Grannies constantly singing or humming unto the Lord. Preoccupy your life with Psalms and hymns and spiritual songs; it will make all the difference in your life.

RELATIVE PRAYER:

Lord, I thank You that many times I am encouraged to sing my prayers to You. Holy Spirit, anoint my prayer, incited by Your Word, that it brings clarity and light for Your will for me.

JOURNAL
A Reflection of Your Thoughts

_____

_____

_____

_____

_____

_____

_____

_____

_____

_____

_____

_____

_____

_____

WEEK TWENTY-EIGHT

NEEDY

No way not to love You. I am so needy and really I had never realized how needy I am. There is no one in this world that can fill everyone's every need, but You, Lord. You fill our need for a Savior, for hope, love, security, faith, purpose, and of course the list goes on and on. Many needs in our lives arise from the many situations or occurrences in our life. Some needs we will never disclose and some we really don't understand ourselves, but You know what they are all about. You tell us that You see even in the darkness. "And not a creature exists that is concealed from His sight, but all things are open and exposed, naked and defenseless to the eyes of Him with Whom we have to do" (Heb. 4:13 AMP).

Lord, You know me, and all of my most secretive needs. You know why we seek to be loved so perfectly, why we need to feel so secure, why we need to be needed, why we need to be so accepted and all those many other needs. I am so glad I can express to You all of my needs. There have been times when I have felt so needy, with only You to really trust with my heart, so I have cried to You with all my soul. Times when I have been desperate to hear Your voice, times I have failed You and needed Your mercy and reassurance, times that I needed You to touch me so I would know You were near. You always fulfill my every need; maybe not the day I call, but there is a day that I acknowledge the need met. I remember the time I was asking You, "Am I following You in the right direction?" and You gave me a vision of me coming out of this building to get in a car. In the dream I questioned whether it was

> *Lord, You know me, and all of my most secretive needs.*

94

the right car. I looked up and the car was an electric car and was hooked to the wiring up above. I knew this was the current of the Holy Spirit. When I awoke I knew You had answered my need. Many times You have answered me through visions and dreams, which speak Your voice to me and really reveal Your heart. I once had a dream about this little toddler who was in her daddy's arms. He was standing and holding her so closely in His arms, but she was still trying to crawl up His chest and get closer, as she cried loudly, "Daddy, Daddy, Daddy!" Like she thought someone was trying to get her. When I awoke the Lord explained to me that I was in the most secure place I could be (in His arms), but still I believed I needed to be closer. I believe that the type of desperation You revealed to me in that dream comes from never wanting to be away from Your care. In our lives we have experienced the not so genuine; we have lost through broken relationships. Our neediness now is because You are the One so perfect that You will always be perfectly needed.

SCRIPTURE FOR MEDITATION:

"By the God of your father who assists you, by El Shaddai who blesses you; with bless-ing of heaven above, blessing of the deep lying below, blessing of breasts and womb, blessing of grain and flowers, blessing of ancient mountains; bounty of the everlasting hills; may they descend on Joseph's head, on the brow of the dedicated one among his brothers" (Genesis 49:25-26 Jerusalem Bible).

WORD FOR THOUGHT:

El Shaddai – *The All-Sufficient One, the God of the mountain, God Almighty – The Many Breasted One.*

MEDITATE ON:

Our neediness is a good thing as I see it, for it is an excellent place for God to reveal Himself in tangible ways to us. Just as He revealed Himself to Abraham as Jehovah Jireh and El Shaddai, in His Presence is where our neediness is richly supplied. Lord, You give us so much.

RELATIVE PRAYER:

Lord, You are well able to supply and nourish my every need. May I seek You always and learn contentment in Your all-sufficient supply.

JOURNAL
A Reflection of Your Thoughts

NO WAY

The question is, will I ever leave you? And the answer is no, no, no. Why? Because I love Him with all my heart and I am so in need of Him. There is no one in this world who can fill anyone's every need, but You Lord. There is no self-sufficiency in my own efforts. The more I have of You the less of everything else I need. I need hope and You supply it, I need purpose and You reveal it, I need faith and you supply it, I need Your love and You give more than I believe is possible. There are so many needy people in the world who are distressed, and they are oblivious to what they need, but I know today that You answer all things. In the Presence of Christ there is no sense of lack. His Presence speaks volumes in the fulfillment of "The Lord is my Shepherd, I shall not want…" (Ps. 23:1 KJV). He fills every nook and cranny, so that the needy can experience His fullest supply. If You would ever leave or discard me (not a chance) there would be nothing or no reason to live on; the only reason I could imagine living on would be to win You back in my life. He became poor, that we the poor might become rich and He became weak that we that are weak might be made strong. Will I ever leave you? No! Someone said, "I searched all over and I couldn't find anything that could compare to you." I needed someone who understood my heart, for I am sure that I myself didn't even understand the movement of my seeking heart. "The heart is hope-

> *I need hope and You supply it, I need purpose and You reveal it, I need faith and you supply it, I need Your love and You give more than I believe is possible.*

lessly dark and deceitful, a puzzle that no one can figure out. But I, God, search the heart and examine the mind. I get to the heart of the human. I get to the root of things. I treat them as they really are, not as they pretend to be" (Jer. 17:9-10 MSG). My neediness needs You.

SCRIPTURE FOR MEDITATION:

"As for me I am poor and needy, yet the Lord takes thought and plans for me: You are my help and my deliverer. O my God, do not tarry!" (Psalm 40:17 AMPC).

WORD FOR THOUGHT:

Needy - *(English) A condition requiring supply or relief; lack; distressed by want of means. (Hebrew) Ebyown- (needy) in the sense of want (especially in feeling); destitute; beggar, needy, poor (man) (Strong's Conc. 34).*

MEDITATE ON:

Reflect on His all-sufficient supply that has been provided for every need you have. Take time to really ponder how many times He brought you out of a dry and thirsty place. Places of brokenness and pain to have laughter again. He is El Shaddai, the All-Sufficient One or the Many Breasted One. Wow! What do you need that He doesn't and can't supply? What could you possibly leave the Lord for?

RELATIVE PRAYER:

Lord, leaving You is not even an option; it is not something to consider even in hard times. Lord, You know that the one thing that would bring me fear is to be separated from You. Please make me know You are near always.

JOURNAL
A REFLECTION OF YOUR THOUGHTS

_____

_____

_____

_____

_____

WEEK THIRTY

FACE TO FACE

Knowing that I'm in His face is quite precarious and certainly more vivid and tangible at different times. I do love it; I appreciate it and honor those precious times. I don't know about everyone else, but I have found for me to get in His face, I (usually) must get out of the face of people. It is exactly when I run from being in the face of people that I walk into this awesome face to face encounter with Him. All by myself, just praising and worshiping, reading and praying bring a true closeness. There is a cliché in the church today about being seeker friendly; to have a "face to face" encounter you must be seeker friendly. What am I talking about? Well, I'm telling you that you must desire this type of friendship with the Lord. The scripture says to be a friend you must show yourself friendly (Prov. 18:24). You can't be friends if you don't like some the same things, agree on the some of the same things and afford the highest level of respect to the person. You can come to the point where as friends, even if disagreeing, you can remain friends, because you agree to disagree, but still respect each other. We remain established friends with The Lord, because of His Person, and we respect that He is right even if we would like to disagree. I remember when David was running from Absalom and Shimei came out and cursed him and threw stones at David. His servant wanted to kill Shimei, but David told him no, because he felt that this was possibly from the Lord, and he didn't want to disagree with anything the Lord desired; he needed to live in the face of God. As the Lord called David to seek His face, He wants us all to seek His face. "You have said, Seek My face [inquire for and require My Presence as your vital need]. My heart says to You, Your face [Your Presence], Lord, will I seek, inquire for, and require [of necessity and on the authority of Your Word]" (Ps. 27:8 AMP). God is able to give you a visitation to turn you toward Him, but we must love His Word to continually behold His face. When we behold His face it's like looking into a mirror that has supernatural power to change our person to the likeness of His Person. "And all of us, as with unveiled face, [because we] continued to behold [in the Word God] as in a mirror the glory of the Lord, are constantly being transfigured into His very own image in ever increasing splendor and from one degree of glory to another; [for this comes] from the Lord [Who is] the Spirit" (2 Cor. 3:18 AMP). His face is the image redesigning our person with each glance; every time you see yourself or say, "That's for me," you can't help but be transformed. When He talks to you to readjust your person you don't get angry, but have such wonderful feelings, just knowing you have His attention. "But don't, dear friend, resent God's discipline; don't sulk under His loving correction. It's the child He loves that God corrects; a Father's delight is behind all this" (Prov. 3: 11-12 MSG). At times you may also experience a hurt feeling. Why? This is because sometimes He magnifies Himself to you to such a degree that you feel undone as you sense the Truth of Who He is. You know that He really deserves so much more than you're able to give. Keep your eyes upon His face. "You are so beautiful to me, can't You see You're everything I hope for, You mean all the world to me, You are so beautiful to me." When you truly fall in love with Him, not just for what He has done for you, you desire to be a person of true beauty, you want to be all that for Him. I want to be a reflection of Him; a reflection of this beauty I'm beholding and sensing. Know that "face to face" means He has chosen you to behold His Person in all His Glory. Truly there should be a humbling and gratefulness that this Great Almighty God would reveal Himself in such a way to you. We should all desire to worship Him in the beauty of holiness. "Up, now slight man! Cast aside now thy burdensome cares, and put away thy toilsome business. Yield room for some little time to God, and rest for a little time in Him. Speak now, my whole heart! Speak now to God, saying I seek Thy face, Thy face, Lord, I will seek" (*The Knowledge of the Holy*, A.W. Tozer). As you get to this point in the "face to face" encounter you must be encouraged to latch on to the faith that declares you to be accepted and loved. You know that you are there only because He Himself wants you before Him. "The Lord hath appeared of old unto me, saying Yea, I have loved thee with an everlasting love: therefore with loving kindness have I drawn thee" (Jer. 31:3 KJV). Remember what He

When we behold His face it's like looking into a mirror that has supernatural power to change our person to the likeness of His Person.

sees of you comes through the radiant face of Christ, who shed His blood for us. You are His chaste, pure, bride, and what splendor, what beauty, and what enjoyment He has in His "face to face" with you. Who is man, that you are so mindful of us? This place, His space, is holy and He alone makes you worthy.

SCRIPTURE FOR MEDITATION:

"And the Lord spake unto Moses face to face as a man speaketh unto his friend, and he said, 'Hear now my words; If there is prophet among you, I the Lord make myself known to him in a vision and speak to him in a dream. But not so with my servant Moses: he is entrusted and faithful in all my house. With him I speak mouth to mouth, clearly and not with dark speeches, and he beholds the form of the Lord. Why then were you not afraid to speak against my servant Moses?'" (Num. 12:6-7 AMP).

WORD FOR THOUGHT:

Radiant – *Radiating rays of light; emitting or reflecting beams of light; vividly shining; glowing, brilliant. Beaming with vivacity and happiness, joy, love, hope, etc.*

MEDITATE ON:

There is a song I believe is by Liddia Ayidia that says, "You are beautiful; with all my heart I cry out; You are so beautiful I'll forever stand in awe; You are so beautiful there is none like You; You are so beautiful and I'll always love You." Think and muse on the beauty you've experienced of your God and King. I read a comment by Charles Wesley in Amplified that said, "Moses, the minister of God, rebukes our partial love ..." Be encouraged to seek His face.

RELATIVE PRAYER:

Lord, surely I know my un-doneness, but I also know You hear my prayers and see my desire to stand before You, and be presented to You as a chaste beautiful virgin. Just as in the time of Queen Esther everything was provided for her to be all the king desired. Lord, I surrender to Your hands. Lord, You are My Potter and I am Your clay.

JOURNAL
A REFLECTION OF YOUR THOUGHTS

_____

_____

_____

_____

_____

_____

_____

_____

_____

_____

_____

_____

_____

_____

_____

RELATIVE READING: "ENCOUNTER" (VISITATION)

It is a beautiful "happening" to encounter the Lord. An encounter is where the Lord chooses to make Himself Personal. It feels so personal that there is the tendency to gloat in self-satisfaction, until you acknowledge truth, "[He] will have mercy on whom [He] will have mercy" (Rom. 9:15 KJV). "God told Moses, 'I'm in charge of mercy. I'm in charge of compassion'" (MSG). Encounters in our lives are indeed His loving kindness toward us. I know that when He gives us an encounter or visitation, He has His own purpose and pleasure for it, although He knows how much we will receive through the encounter. An encounter with the Lord can leave you spellbound and surely overwhelmed, according to the type He gives. One of the things I received from my first encounter was this absolute reality of truth that pertained to everything I knew and didn't know about God. The truth of Him vibrated through my being. I knew that I had encountered the True and Living God. Why? Well, there is this feel of saturated holiness surrounding you and you know this is Him. This is an intriguing or mind-blowing reality; you think, "Who am I that this Vast, Awesome God, who controls the whole of everything would take time to show Himself to me?" Encounters keep you strife-less with men; you don't waste precious time with such, because nothing will stop you from encountering Him again. You know this is not about men, but about God, so you live and enjoy relationship with Him, and relationship is the best assurance you will have another encounter. Can I say to you that every encounter that I have had was never my going after an encounter, but going passionately after Him. "When a man's attention is undivided, than God's attention is commanded" (Unknown). I have tried not to have a problem with believing Him to be and do the same that His Word reveals about Him. All that people say they believe God did in scripture they don't believe Him to do in this day. In fact, you will probably hear them say, "Lord, I want this if it is at all possible for me," and "if it be Your will." They believe they are following the example of Jesus, but Jesus' time on this earth explicitly demanded the Word be fulfilled. When it comes to the cross He had to ask, "If it be possible let this cup pass from me." Because He already knew what was written, He humbled Himself and said, "Not my will, but Your will be done." His Word is always His will. An encounter with God is impossible to many, but we must deny our opinions and consider only the scriptures; when it does not violate the Word it's possible even for our day. The scriptures speak of and agree with encounters with the Lord and with angels. This is not only found in the Old Testament, but also in the New Testament, which we are still in. I am amazed at how many times we read that the children of Israel encountered a tangible appearance of the Living God and at how many times even encounters with angels are in scripture. Encounters can offend and contradict our natural make up. Encounters are not given because you give Him permission, but as He sees the need or desire. Encounters with angels are powerful but will never be as overwhelming as an encounter with the Lord, unless it is with the identified angels in scripture, Gabriel and Michael, who pronounce themselves angels that stand in direct proximity of the Lord. These two carry an overwhelming presence; this type of presence caused Daniel to fall as a dead man as Gabriel spoke to Him. With an encounter you know the exact day and time of the happening, for it is a special experience. An encounter is "vivified," endued with life; it quickens you and it seems to be as an animated happening. It is an experience

Every encounter that I have had was never my going after an encounter, but going passionately after Him.

that captures a place in your memory forever and carries the power of change for all of us. Encounters are electrifying and leave you with the sense of a personal relationship, usually tagged with feelings of intimacy. Encounters always reveal His nature in some manner (holiness, love, mercy). I will say encounters cause you to dream bigger. You will see the need, as scripture encourages us, to "enlarge your tent, stretch forth, lengthen, strengthen and spare not" (Isa. 54:2). "Clear lots of ground for your tents! Make your tents large. Spread out! Think big! Use plenty of rope, drive the tent pegs deep" (MSG). All encounters enlarge you in some capacity. Prophetic Word: "Walk with me, keep pace with Me! Walk with Me, keep pace with Me; Walk with Me, keep pace with Me, as Enoch walked with Me and kept pace with Me. These are last times. As you walk with Me and keep pace with Me I will show you My end time happening for this hour, those things that you don't understand and know. Things that are fenced in, but ready to be revealed in this time. These things carry with them the revelation of the sons of God. Remember Enoch was and then he was not, because he pleased Me. Remember Elijah and Elisha; Elisha was determined to stick with Elijah. Everywhere Elijah went Elisha kept pace with him. He refused to be a moment behind Elijah and received not just what Elijah had, but a double portion. Walk with Me, talk with Me, keep pace with Me, keep pace with Me! There will be a manifestation of the sons of God; they are those who want more. Know that your faithfulness, determination, steadfastness and desire are from Me. I quicken you to be diligent that you might show forth My Name." People who have had encounters with the Living God seem always to be bold with a personal constitution not to deny the teaching of their God. They seem for the most part to believe in their identity and authority. The Apostles were said to have all been martyred except for one; I ask myself how could they have stayed so true to their faith even to death. I do believe their encounters with the Lord subsequently had a lot to do with their boldness even unto death. "But he, being full of the Holy Ghost, looked up steadfastly into heaven, and saw the glory of God, and Jesus standing at the right hand of God" (Acts 7:55 KJV). "But Stephen, full of the Holly Spirit, hardly noticed- he only had eyes for God, whom he saw in all His glory with Jesus standing at His side. He said, 'Oh! I see heaven wide open and the Son of Man standing at God's side!'" (MSG). The father of faith had encounters with God. The scripture says in Genesis 18:23, "And Abraham came close and said ..." Really, God appeared to him in an Omni-Body; God had taken a body to get close to Abraham to talk to him. W.O.W. Oh, the possibility that the Lord would avail us this type of attention is truly something that makes my prayers to Him even more of an investment. We thank the Lord for the excitement of possibility.

WEIGHT OF HIS LOVE

Lord! It never fails. When I'm in Your Presence for a good amount of time this condensed weight of Your love is felt and released in waves. I remember asking You, "Why does this happen when I read and meditate on Your Word? Why do I begin to sense Your great love for me and Your power? You made me know that when I love Your Word and muse on it, I'm loving You. You then oblige Yourself to love me back in power and love. (The Word was with God and the Word was God.) Your love is exuberating, refreshing, and excellent in every way." Just to abide in this place of love for a time really does compel you to want to tell someone or help someone to understand the dimensions of His great love (breadth, length, depth, and height). You understand that He has the capability to show you superabundantly above what you can ask or even think of His wonderful love (Eph. 3:18). When His love is being projected in this way there will be things that work against this precious time, a phone call or a thought of something you need to do, something to disturb this place. Did you know that you can actually cut the phone off? We have missed out when we come to church and are more aware of our phones than the word that is being ministered. There was a time we did not have this distraction and God always kept things in order until we could get home and find out who wanted our attention. Help us, Lord, to be determined that nothing will negate this time. Shut out, shut down, and shut off everything but Him, and the reward will be so expressive and intensive and weighty. You will find yourself yielding increase that can only be attributed to abiding under this weight of love, Presence and glory. Can I tell you that it is not the works of righteousness that change us, but knowing and experiencing this weighty love. So many are always trying to be in the presence of people and really have nothing to contribute but a lot of big words. If you learn to stay in God's Presence, when God sends you among people you will have real substance, right from the heart of God, and it will be weighty. I listen to some ministers and I'm not trying to judge anyone, but I hear barrenness and know that they don't have to be that way, if they would just spend time with His Person. He gives you personal touches that you know come from His Person; it's just you and His extreme love. When I say personal touches I mean His touch is according to what He knows you need. You try your best to render to Him a recompense of love, tears of thanksgiving and joy, but everything seems inadequate, and everything you express doesn't equate to His inexpressibleness. I just explain

Shut out, shut down, and shut off everything but Him, and the reward will be so expressive and intensive and weighty.

it as a heavy weight of His glorious love that is consuming. I was reading a book that related this comment by John Tennant as he experienced the weightiness of His Glory. "Hold, Lord, it is enough! Or the frail vessel will break beneath the weight of glory." There is no way to recompense this weight of love. We must receive and cherish this weight of His love with all out appreciation, and the Holy Spirit will delight to draw us again and again to His place.

SCRIPTURE FOR MEDITATION:

"May He grant you out of the rich treasury of His glory to be strengthened and reinforced with mighty power in the inner man by the Holy Spirit Himself indwelling your innermost being and personality. May Christ through your faith dwell (settle down, abide, make His permanent home) in your hearts. May you be rooted deep in love and founded securely on love that you may have the power and be strong to apprehend and grasp with all the saints (God's devoted people) the experience of that love, what is the breadth and length and height and depth of it" (Ephesians 3:16 AMP).

WORD FOR THOUGHT:

Weight – *"Baros" prob. from 922 (through the notion of going down; weight; in the N.T. only fig. a load, abundance, authority; burden, extent, mystery, depth (deepness) (Strong's Conc.).*

MEDITATE ON:

More love, more power, more of Christ in your life. Meditate on the weightiness of His person, His abundance, His love and the treasures of mysteries of His Person revealed by His Word. This can take your breath away.

RELATIVE PRAYER:

Lord, weigh down on us in the Person of Your love- breathe on us. Let us experience the copiousness of Your fullness. Lord, as Paul's desire, so is our desire to know You.

JOURNAL
A Reflection of Your Thoughts

_____

_____

_____

_____

_____

_____

_____

_____

_____

_____

_____

_____

_____

Week Thirty-Two

TANGIBLE

While in Your Presence I am mesmerized by how well you can relate Your Person to us. I believe it all has to do with leaving self (flesh) and entering and abiding in the Spirit. Spirit to spirit is the nucleus that sets off the right energy into our atmosphere, bringing Tangible Presence. This Tangible Presence can be perceived and understood to the point that new levels of communication become recognizable. Communication, I've often heard, is the essence of every relationship. Lord, I know You desire communication with us, because Your dealings with man in every dispensation confirm this. In the Garden of Eden, You wanted communication, in the Tabernacle You wanted communication, the Ephod was all about communication, the prophets are about communication, You sent Your son to communicate with us. Emmanuel is the one who dwelled with us, and now the Holy Spirit is our constant communication in Your things. The Holy Spirit is the Master Communicator; He is here to communicate the Person and Glory of Jesus to us. I once had a dream that I was skipping across the map of the United States and I realized that this Man's son was with me, and I asked Him if He wanted to turn around and not go with me across the map? He told me He had no intention of leaving me. I knew immediately when I awoke that the Holy Spirit had revealed and settled the Son's intention to be Present with me. I knew He would not leave me or forsake me, but His Presence would go with me. I believe I understood the dream immediately because when you spend lot of time (abide) in the Presence of our Lord then the Holy Spirit can present in our spirit the reality of His Person communing with us. In this way His ways are seeable, touchable, and felt. Lord, of course You are desirous to communicate Your tan-

109

gible Person, but so many of Your people are given to vanities. This is not conducive for our communicating, Spirit to spirit with the Lord. These vanities stop the flow of Spirit to spirit. When we talk about vanities this is what we are talking about: lack of worth, useless things, empty things, things of no true value, excessive pride. There is only one part of the make-up of man that is capable of hearing You and that is not the pride of man, but it is our spirit man, quickened by the Holy Spirit so You could admonish us, speak to us, in our quickened state. You want and are able to enjoy our spirit as it has been quickened. It is in the spirit that we can relate to a Tangible Personal Lord, Who is Spirit. Oh, people of God, know that it is and was always meant to be Spirit to spirit.

> *This Tangible Presence can be perceived and understood to the point that new levels of communication become recognizable.*

SCRIPTURE FOR MEDITATION:

"The grace (favor and spiritual blessing) of the Lord Jesus Christ and the love of God and the presence and the fellowship (the communion and sharing together, and participation) in the Holy Spirit be with you all. Amen (so be it)" (2 Corinthians 13:14 AMP).

WORD FOR THOUGHT:

Communion – *"koinonia:" partnership i.e. (lit) participation, or social intercourse or benefaction- (to) communicate (-ation), distribution, fellowship. From 2844 'Koinonos:" a sharer; companion, fellowship, partaker, partner. (2842, 2944 Strong's Conc.).*

MEDITATE ON:

All the different vanities (emptiness, idleness, useless lies) you need to inhibit, so your spirit won't be inhibited from communing with the Spirit of God. Decide today to say no to and restrain anything that neutralizes Spirit to spirit.

RELATIVE PRAYER:

Oh Lord! I appreciate a tangible relationship with You. My spirit perceives Your Spirit indulging in conversation with one (me) who doesn't deserve it, but I truly prize it above all. Lord, I want to live as worthily as I can of the privilege of open lines of communication with Your Spirit.

JOURNAL

A Reflection of Your Thoughts

_____

_____

_____

_____

_____

_____

_____

_____

_____

_____

_____

_____

_____

_____

_____

_____

_____

_____

_____

HOW DARE THEY?

Your Presence, Your anointing, is forever a movement cherished in our lives. To watch You work in and through others and myself, the sure wonder of the things You do at any given moment. How dare anyone think what comes from mere men and women is a product of their own doing? I know I have nothing, we have nothing to give, but You who live inside us. There are many things I must do, but spending time in Your Presence is by far the most valuable thing anyone can do. David expounded that a day in the courts of the Lord is better than a thousand anywhere else. Lord, it is You that makes us who we are. Paul says, "I am what I am, but by the grace of God." The Apostles made clear in Acts that spending time with You was the most valuable thing they did. Yes, giving themselves to You, Lord, was more profitable to them than the business of the day. "But we will continue to devote ourselves steadfastly to prayer and the ministry of the word" (Acts 6:4 AMP). As we linger in Your Presence there is a felt infusion. At times we feel different happenings: joy, a pressing into the greater things of the kingdom, power seeming to surge in us, Your authority rising in our lives. These and many more things take place. There was a song we sang some years back that said, "More love and more prayer is more of You in our lives." I'm a witness that this is true. It is this infusion of Your Person that allows us to impart into the lives of men and women who need to receive from the Person of Christ, not man. It is sure ludicrous to think that flesh can heal the sick, raise the dead, or give sight to the blind. The flesh must be brought down and rebuked if it ever gravitates to glory in anything but Christ. The Lord is serious when He says that to live through His life we must die. "He that loveth father or mother more than me is not worthy of me: and he that loveth son or daughter more than me is not worthy of me. And he that taketh not his cross, and followeth after me is not worthy of me. And he that findeth his life shall lose it: and he that loseth his life for my sake shall find it" (Matt. 10:37-39 KJV). The inconstancy of living sometimes in and sometimes out is a great hindrance to all God can do and wants to do to bring Glory to His Name. The flesh is a stickler in satisfying its craving to live high. This is promoted through the lust of the eye, lust of the flesh, and the pride of life. We must build up our spirit man for it is the spirit man that longs to wait before His lovely face to be infused by the glory promised even before the flesh came into existence. It is the spirit man that craves, must have, Your Presence to Be. Lord, it is Your Person You infuse into us that brings forth such marvelous happenings. Surely it is of Your fullness that we partake. How dare anyone think mere men can be responsible for Your glory?

> *It is sure ludicrous to think that flesh can heal the sick, raise the dead, or give sight to the blind.*

SCRIPTURE FOR MEDITATION:

"So the twelve convened the multitude of the disciples and said, it is not seemly or right that we should have to give up or neglect the Word of God in order to attend to serving at tables and superintending the distribution of food ... but we will continue to devote ourselves steadfastly to prayer and the ministry of the Word" (Acts 6:2-4 AMPC).

WORD FOR THOUGHT:

Infusion – *to pour into or in; introduce, usu. by power; to include; instill; the act of infusing; that which is infused. (The Living Webster Enc. Dict.).*

MEDITATE ON:

The Lord living within you, and every day spend time with Him meditating in His Word, musing on His fullness. You should know your capacity for Him enlarges itself as He expands His domain in you. More of everything: His mercy, compassion, holiness, power, wisdom, etc. Beware not to think of yourself more highly than you ought, and thank Him for Him.

RELATIVE PRAYER:

Lord, we do desire to be used by You for Your kingdom. Let us never desire our glory, but humble ourselves in Your Presence continually.

JOURNAL

A Reflection of Your Thoughts

_____

_____

_____

_____

_____

_____

_____

_____

_____

_____

_____

_____

_____

_____

_____

_____

_____

_____

_____

_____

BETRAYED BY YOUR SPEECH

Your words betray the truths in your life. Those who live in His Presence talk differently than those who just come in contact with the Presence now and then. "As in water face answers to and reflects face, so the heart of man to man" (Prov. 27:19 AMPC). "Just as water mirrors your face, so your face mirrors you heart" (MSG). Whatever is in your heart will be revealed from your speech. Jesus said, "Out of the abundance of the heart the mouth speaketh" (Matt. 12:34 KJV). "... For the mouth speaks what overflows from the heart" (CJB). We know David was a mighty warrior; he was a defender of the Lord's Name and His honor. His speech betrays his love for God, the compelling reason for his actions. "One thing have I desired (asked) of the lord, that will I seek, inquire for, and (insistently) require: that I may dwell in the house of the Lord [in His Presence] all the days of my life, to behold and gaze upon the beauty [the sweet attractiveness and the delightful loveliness] of the Lord, and to meditate, consider, and inquire in His temple" (Ps. 27:4 AMP). David's speech revealed that he had knowledge of God's matchless beauty, which can only be captured by throne room encounters. "In Your Presence is fullness of joy, at your right hand pleasures forevermore" (Ps. 16:11 AMP). "As the heart pants and longs for the water brooks, so I pant and long for You, O God. My inner self thirsts for God, for the Living God" (Ps. 42:1-2 AMP). This is a person who has truly encountered the Presence of the Lord, which is worth fighting for. These people who abide in His Presence will generally personalize their conversation with and about the

Lord. They assert themselves in their relationship with God, for they know nothing can satisfy but more Presence. "Faith is an organ of knowledge, and love is an organ for experience" (Tozer). These words can only come from one who sought and entered into this heart transition of Divine Presence. The words one speaks actually amaze that person to the point they know the Holy Spirit has given them the ability to express the mysteries of being in His Presence. There are truly mysterious things that happen in your person when you seek to avail yourself to His Person. You need to know there can be a transition or turning from your person to a total embrace of His Person. Your identity is no longer the prevailing thing. I was driving toward the mountains and noticing how huge and majestically beautiful they were. The Lord and I began to converse about His Greatness and I began to attribute my worth to Him. I heard myself say, "Who am I, but You?" Those words came bubbling out of my innermost spirit that day, as I opened my mouth expressing what I was feeling about myself in respect to my Lord. It was the Holy Spirit who had given me those words to express the richness of my position with the Lord. This identity, this richness can only be found in the loss of our self-identity. It will always take the Holy Spirit to reveal and express the treasures of what you gain in His Presence. "And after a while came unto him they that stood by, and said to Peter, Surely thou also art one of them; for thy speech betrayeth thee" (Matt. 26:73 KJV).

> *Those who live in His Presence talk differently than those who just come in contact with the Presence now and then.*

… Linen in which the housewife has laid rosemary and lavender will smell fragrantly; ordinary iron placed near a magnet becomes magnetic; those that are in king's courts catch a refined and courteous mien; the friend of wise men gets wisdom; the members of a closely-knit family contract by association some tiny gesture, a peculiarity which betrays their oneness; it is proverbial how on the faces of an aged couple there is seen a strong resemblance so that each reflects the other. And it is impossible for us to be much with God without becoming godly, God-like (F.B. Meyer).

Don't be fooled. Your speech will betray you, whether you abide in His Presence or not.

SCRIPTURE FOR MEDITATION:

"Give ear, O heavens, and I (Moses) will speak; and let the earth hear the words of

my mouth. My message shall drop as the rain, my speech shalt distil as the dew, as the light rain upon the tender grass, and as the showers upon the herb. For I will proclaim the name [and presence] of the Lord. Concede and ascribe greatness to our God" (Deuteronomy 32:1-3 AMPC).

WORD FOR THOUGHT:

Speech *– Act or manner of speaking; communication or expression of thoughts in spoken words; that which is spoken; uttered words expressive of thought (Webster's Dict.).*

MEDITATE ON:

What your speech might project. Does your speech project time spent in His Presence? Association breeds assimilation and you can expect that your person will change, also your speech. Some people's speech reveals their enrollment in the systems of this world. (They know everything about this entire world of "superstars.") Don't ask them what the message was yesterday. They haven't entertained it long enough to remember it. This speech is not a forced thing; it just happens when you've been with Jesus. It is your speech that has a proclivity to reveal the beauty of His Person.

RELATIVE PRAYER:

Lord, let my words reveal the Christ who lives in me.

JOURNAL
A Reflection of Your Thoughts

WEEK THIRTY-FIVE

IN-TO-ME SEE

Lord, you have told us to pray without ceasing. This is a blessed challenge. As I drive down the street and freeway I pray for whatever the Spirit quickens me about. Being obedient to the Holy Spirit is the best way to fulfill this command. I know and see so many people, and I seem to feel their pain. While watching the news I find many things to pray for. Prayer for a believer should be our habitual mode of operation. We are co-partners with God to bring His kingdom to this earth, as were Daniel, Elijah and others. There are many different prayer types and all are necessary, but there is a prayer that You have designated for my personal life and relationship with You. You desire it for every believer, and I simply describe it as the prayer of intimacy. It is by far the most patient and unrushed prayer in my life. This prayer carries much time for just musing on Your Person. It is also in this prayer time that my soul reaches for and inhabits the deeper relational places with You. You give this time of prayer to anyone who is thirsting to know and see Your Person. "For He willeth that we be occupied in knowing and loving," wrote Julian of Norwich, "Till the time that we shall be fulfilled in heaven …" (*Knowledge of the Holy*, A.W. Tozer). This prayer of intimacy takes me soaring past problems, situations, people, business and ministry. You lose attachment to the earthly, and go to the place of desire and pleasure where He meets you in rare form. "But when the Holy Ghost shows us God as He is we admire Him to the point of wonder and delight" (A.W. Tozer). You begin to sense all of these good and special things about Him and your relationship with Him. You can come to this prayer feeling tears and weariness, but as you focus on adoring His beautiful Person, you can be relieved of any weariness or useless feeling. Sometimes you just flow into this prayer and sometimes you are pressed to enter it. You can't confuse this prayer of intimacy with any other prayer, because the Lord makes it clear that they won't mesh. This unadulterated prayer is all about Him and you, how much He means to you and how much you mean to Him. This is you purposefully taking time to be alone with Him without any intrusion. Lord, I always know I'm in this time, because it is so pleasurable; it's a soft and amorous prayer. This prayer is not ambitious, but completing and satisfying. Some might ask the necessity of this prayer time; just know that you will surely enjoy

> *Sometimes you just flow into this prayer and sometimes you are pressed to enter it.*

this prayer, but I also believe it is the panting of His heart to have this personal unadulterated time with us. I love the way Israel Houghton expressed this time in lyrics of one of his songs: "Away, away from the noise, alone with you; away, away to hear Your voice and meet with You; nothing else matters, my one desire is to worship you." Paul says, "but God hath revealed them unto us by His Spirit: for the Spirit searcheth all things, yea, the deep things of God. For what man knoweth the things of a man, save the spirit of man which is in him? Even so the things of God knoweth no man, but the Spirit of God" (1 Cor. 2:10-11 KJV). Spending time intimately with God will be the place where the Spirit can allow you to "In-to-Me-See" God.

SCRIPTURE FOR MEDITATION:

"My beloved speaks and says to me, rise up, my love, my fair one, and come away. For, behold, the winter is past; the rain is over and gone. The flowers appear on the earth; the time of the singing {birds} has come, and the voice of the turtledove is heard in our land. The fig tree puts forth and ripens her green figs, and the vines are in blossom and give forth their fragrance. Arise, my love, my fair one, and come away" (SOS 2:10-13 AMPC).

WORD FOR THOUGHT:

Intimacy – *Familiarity, marked by very close association or contact, suggesting informal warmth or privacy, of a very personal or private nature.*

MEDITATE ON:

Your desire to get away with just you and the Lord. Are you anxious? Are you anticipating this time? Who wouldn't want to come away after hearing the words He spoke in SOS 2:10-13? Intimacy is always a place of fruitfulness. Times of intimate prayer birth dreams and visions, and are infused with power, with His likeness and wisdom. All of these will make their entry into your life, because of the prayer of intimacy.

RELATIVE PRAYER:
Lord, that I may know You, as I am known by You, in whatever way I am able.

JOURNAL
A REFLECTION OF YOUR THOUGHTS

_____

_____

_____

_____

_____

_____

_____

_____

_____

_____

_____

_____

_____

_____

_____

_____

RELATIVE READING: "GLORY"

Today in Christendom true believers realize that we have allowed decades to go by without truly seeking the one thing we have only heard about in times gone past. Thank God He has brought us to the time when the buzzwords, or can I say the words being filtered through the church are "His Presence" and "His Glory." Surely many of us have heard about times of great revival and true releases of glory in the different moves of God. I believe we have come to a time when we who are truly after God, and not just the things and the blessing of God, will not be satisfied with anything less than His Glory released in our lives. We want it in meetings and gatherings, so people will be captivated and subjugated only to Christ. What are we looking for? What are we longing for? Is it for this time? What is the difference in people who experienced this glory in the past and people now? Will God again send a move of His Glory for this time? There are so many questions we could ask, but the fact we first need to settle in our mind is, "Yes! He will send a move of His Glory in this time." I believe this latter time, according to scripture and tracing His pattern of doing things, seems to me the appointed time when He will send the Greater Glory. "The first shall be last and the last shall be first" (Lk. 13:30 KJV). The best seems to be saved for last (Jn. 2:10). "The glory of the latter house shall be greater than that of the former" (Hag. 2:9 KJV). "To Him be glory in the church and in Christ Jesus throughout all generations, forever and ever! Amen" (Eph. 3:21 ESV). "Arise, shine, for your light has come, and the glory of the Lord rises upon you. See, darkness covers the earth and thick darkness is over the peoples, but the Lord rises upon you and His glory appears over you" (Is. 60:1-2 NIV). We believe that we have entered the time of the latter rains. This is the time of the greatest harvest. Greater harvest puts a demand on greater Glory. By far this must be the greatest time in the history of man for the accumulation and culmination of the Glory before the coming of the Prince of Peace (Yeshua). I believe God will put groups of people together that will be in harmony with His purpose and Person. People with childlike faith; not those who consider themselves intellectual and deep, but those who like to keep it simple. Simple, like loving His Word and just wanting Him. Know that those who love His word enjoy passionately, simply praising and worshiping Him in childlike faith. The Glory is rising! When we give full worship to Him for Who He is and for His Goodness we will see the Glory. As we read in 2 Chronicles chapter 5:13 and 14, then again in 2 Chronicles 7:1 and 2:

> It came even to pass, as the trumpeters and singers were as one, to
> make one sound to be heard in praising and thanking the Lord, and
> when they lifted up their voice with the trumpets and cymbals and

instruments of music, and praised the Lord, saying, for He is good; for His mercy endureth for ever: that then the house was filled with a cloud, even the house of the Lord; So that the priests could not stand to minister by reason of the cloud: for the glory of the Lord had filled the House of God ... Now when Solomon had made an end of praying, the fire came down from heaven, and consumed the burnt offering and sacrifices, and the glory of the Lord filled the house. And the priests could not enter into the house of the Lord, because the glory of the Lord had filled the Lord's house. And when all the children of Israel saw how the fire came down, and the glory of the Lord upon the house, they bowed themselves with their faces to the ground upon the pavement, and worshiped, and praised the Lord, saying, for He is good; for His mercy endureth for ever.

When a house fills up with Glory it has no room for anything else. Every atmosphere is not conducive for glory. When our sacrificial offerings are accepted of God, there is an excellent chance that His Glory will fill the place.

When we become so intrigued with His Person (not just His blessing) we will want to see into His Splendor.

———

Earlier we asked the question, "To what types of people will God reveal His Glory?" I believe it is the longing, passionate, needy, desperate and sold out, (all on the altar) people who are after the Heart of God. They have made up their minds, nothing else will do; we find this desiring, longing, and needy remnant crying out to The God of Glory, "Show me Your Glory." I don't believe it takes everyone (if it is everyone, that would be the perfect setting), but a core of determined people. These are excerpts from F.B. Meyer's book, *Moses*. "The desire to see God carries with it the pledge of its gratification ... During long years the desire had been growing in the heart of Moses to see the face of God ... Show me now thy way, that I may know Thee ... I beseech Thee, show me Thy glory." Prayers like these were constantly on his lips. And sometimes with him, as with saints of later days, the yearning must have become almost too intense to be borne. No invalid in dark cold winter days so longs for summer; no true heart so longs for its mate; no young bride just widowed so longs for the everlasting reunion of heaven, as do some saintly hearts long for God. But these longings are certain to be fulfilled, because God is faithful. Some will ask what we could possibly be asking for. We're saved, have food on our table, have nice cars and homes; our ministries are doing good things for the glory of God. To this question I will refer you to Moses when he asked God to show him His Glory. Moses had seen it all; so many miracles, can we even name them all? God talked to Moses face to face, Moses saw a similitude of the Lord when he talked to God. What possibly could Moses still be asking for? Moses had seen the acts of His Glory. All that God had showed him intrigued Moses, and because God had showed him so much; with full desire there was a longing to experience the Person of Glory, He Himself. What am I talking about? We are asking God to show Himself, the Living Presence of His Person. When we become so intrigued with His Person (not just His blessing) we will want to see into His Splendor (brilliancy; magnificence; pomp; glory; grandeur; eminence). We know we can't stand under all His weight (this is not craziness), but we want to see into His Copious Splendor. Truly His acts of Glory we want in our midst, but like Moses we also want to know Glory, the feel of Glory, which is none other than He Himself. We want to touch more of Him, His glory lying on us or weighing on us until there is no doubt this is His Person, Him covering us in Glory.

One definition of Glory in the Hebrew is "Kabed" (heavyweight). I know many won't understand all we are trying to say now, but keep on seeking Him and you will come to the place where words can't express what you're trying to say and yet you know what you want to say. Even as Moses had experienced the Shekinah many times, he asked God for more and He gave it to him. He told us in Jeremiah 33:3, "Call to Me and I will answer you and show you great and mighty things, fenced in and hidden, which you do not know - do not distinguish and recognize, have knowledge of and understand" (AMP). I did a word study on the words great and mighty, and these are just a few of the definitions I found: exceeding, more, much, proud things, noble, made large with honor, excellent, inaccessible, fenced in or fortified, isolated. We must realize He wants to show us these things that reference the splendor of His Person. Have I ever experienced this Glory that I'm still seeking and talking about? I have experienced the "Shekinah" and the "Kabed" which is amazing to the finiteness of man. It was just a glimpse, a passing feeling, a slight suggestion or an inkling of the weight of His Person, but you know that it is Him in His Glory. He is ever so careful to give us no more than we can handle. Let us use the Hebrew expression that is used many times for Glory, "Shekinah." The Shekinah is expeditiously tangible; it is expeditiously special in every way, and you have no desire to hold on to the natural (your activity ceases), for the glorious and heavenly is surrounding you and you know it. The Lord is moving and working and who would dare to oppose Him? The "Shekinah" leaves you absolutely dependent on, yielded to the Holy Spirit in a most vulnerable way, knowing that what is next will come from Him. What you're seeing and experiencing is tangible glory. The "Kabed" is beauty moving at its best, glorious and mystical. It is a place that no one could have convinced you exists. You feel somewhat mesmerized, but you immediately acknowledge His Person, because nothing or no One could do this to you, but Him. It is like a heavy weight on your person that comes with a fullness of love and His determined desire that you know Him in His fullness. His "Kabed" has the ability to overwhelm your finiteness. The "Kabed" and the "Shekinah" are personal, even if you're in a corporate gathering. It affects you personally; to experience this is without question the privilege of a lifetime. I don't know everyone's experience with the "Shekinah", and I know "Shekinah" can be released any way God desires.

One of my experiences with His "Shekinah," with "Kabed," came as waves, overwhelming waves of the ocean. Each wave you feel has the capacity to over-whelm you, but there is still this sheer delight that comes with it, penetrating your whole person. There is a slight fear, but if you are drowning the beauty of it all is that you're with Him and it's breathtaking. You don't know how this could be happening to you, but you know this is God. Once at our conference "Beyond the Veil Encounter," the Glory came in just as the speaker was closing the message. They gave me the mike and there was nothing I could say; I fell to the floor and begin to experience this rapturous pleasure. It was covering and submerging me. Truly you can't minister when that thick and heavy Glory comes in. If everyone is experiencing this they don't care an iota what you have to say at this point, because they are before Him and He has all their atten-tion. If you asked me what brought this kind of Shekinah and Kabed into the Encounter, I really have no confirmed answer. This is what I believe; the people didn't come for a lot of hype, but were hungry and came expecting to meet Jesus (Yeshua), not some great personalities, but Him. The whole Encounter was focused on an atmosphere to encounter Him with all He would give us of Himself. As the speaker gave me the mike she said, "Do you want to go Behind the Veil? There it is. Go." Now the speaker was talking about going behind our set for the Encounter, for there were curtains, and behind the curtains was the Ark of the Covenant. With those words the people of God jumped out of their seats and began literally to run as if they were in a race. You would have believed that there was a million dollars behind our set. I watched two ladies running like "I will get there first." The children were running to get "Behind the Veil"; I could see them behind the curtains praising, worshiping, crying, and speak-ing in their heavenly language. As I saw our children with their hands up the "Shekinah" was falling in waves. As I said, I was given the mike and could not minister, but fell to the floor and for a time could not get up, as waves of Glory came in a steady flow. What do you do in this kind of "Shekinah?" Nothing, just receive, for the Shekinah controls the atmosphere. We were having the event at a hotel and really went somewhat over our time. The "Shekinah" with the "Kabed" (they will come together; I believe this was one of such times that He brings the glory, as the former and the latter rains) leaves you weaker, but fully satisfied and completed. You always believed you could live for Him forever, but now you know you will live for Him forever. There are such feelings of joy, satisfaction and completion and still yet always knowing there is so much more of Him; it's like those waves of the ocean. Who can contain them? He can't be exhausted. Anything holy and good can happen in the glory, innumerous things.

Now to close this, I want to tell you what I feel will keep us in the ballpark for His Glory. I heard someone say that there are keys to His revealed Glory and I agree with these. One: hunger, an insatiable appetite for God Himself. Two: listening to the Holy Spirit and pressing in His direction. Passion will keep you in hot pursuit (willing to go farther, even to walk on the water). Three: you must stand in faith, without losing your hunger and your press, when it doesn't happen when you think it should. Four: live a pure life, love His holiness and hold it in great reverence, without holiness no man shall see the Lord. Five: believe He wants to show you His Glory: (it's His desire to reveal Himself). Know that it is the Blood of Jesus (Yeshua) and the cross that gives us a right and the privilege to know Him in all His Glory; we can draw nigh to His Person and Glory. Remember the atmosphere is not conducive in every place and every one will not be able to go where you go, not because God doesn't desire to be there (Shammah). Why? I believe these might be some of the major problems: One: man's glory dominates, two: carnality (self pleasure), third: attractions to the worldly promotions and four: absence of love which is the cohesive to unity. Anyone who has experienced any portion of His Glory will be delivered from seeking the glory of man, for there is no comparison and no match. The things we highly valued will take a different position in our lives, and we know that the Glory humbles the flesh. When we value nothing greater than Him we will continue to seek to know what is possible; what can I know about You and Your Glory? We will never know unless we seek Him with all of our hearts and with the Holy Spirit leading we will find what we seek, "The Glory."

OVERDRIVE

Lord, I have no desire whatsoever to do ministry without Your Presence. It is only in Your Presence that I feel capable. I know You are with me always, but when I am personally involved with Your Personal Presence I feel I am capable of overdrive. In years past I was troubled with insecurity; I was a "scaredy-cat," always wondering about my insufficiencies, allowing them to amaze me and hinder my progress. The boldness that is generated from within is amazing, because of You within. I now always enjoy the sheltering of Your Person, because the Holy Spirit has taught me to be mindful of Your Presence. I know that at any given time there are legions of angels available for Your purpose. I know that I win, I overcome, I conquer, I am the victor and I am excited about ministry. Surely the cry of Moses' heart is the cry of my heart, "Carry me not up hence, if Your Personal Presence go not with me. I want You surrounding me, I want You in me, and through me, can't go nowhere without You." I ponder David's words, in Psalm 18:17, "He delivered me from my strong enemy, and from them which hated me; for they were too strong for me." David truly makes clear that his victory was because of You Lord. Then he says, "For by Thee I have run

Overdrive is my total reliance on the Holy Spirit that gives me an overflow to operate from.

through a troop; and by my God have I leaped over a wall." We see David operating in overdrive because You were the energy in his life. You make the difference in our lives. I must live under Your wings. I recognize that overdrive is that higher level of zeal, unction, and power. When people begin to respond to me I know they are responding to Your Presence. Overdrive is my total reliance on the Holy Spirit that gives me an overflow to operate from. Just a wave of a hand over any person with expectation, and of course the laying on of hands reveals Your Presence in and through and all around my being. My awareness and my mindfulness of Your Presence give a sense of changing gears and going into overdrive; I always ask You, "What are You planning on doing with this release?" There is no greater joy, no greater completeness and fulfillment for my life than the overdrive I feel at this moment. At this point you recognize that you are totally under the Diocese of His Presence, The Holy Spirit. You don't shift gears, He does; you are sheltered by His Presence and under His jurisdiction. The Holy Spirit can take us for the ride of our lives. I believe it is His sheer delight, for He is here to reveal the Son as the Son revealed the Father and His glory.

SCRIPTURE FOR MEDITATION:

"You are the One Who lights my lamp. 'The Lord my God illumines my darkness. With You I can charge into battle; With You I can leap over a wall'" (Psalm 18:28-29 CEB).

"Suddenly, God, You floodlight my life; I'm blazing with glory, God's Glory! I smash the bands of marauders, I vault the highest fences" (MSG).

WORD FOR THOUGHT:

Overflow – *To flow or spread over; to inundate; to cause to run over the brim of; to deluge; to overwhelm—To swell and run over the brim or banks; to be so full that the contents run over; to abound; a flowing over; superabundance (The Living Webster p. 675).*

MEDITATE ON:

Living in Him and through Him, living by Him and for Him. Let Him see out of your eyes and speak from your mouth and touch through your hands, as you live in the overflow of His Person on overdrive.

RELATIVE PRAYER:

Lord, that I may trust in You and You alone. Never allow me to be secure in myself or anyone or anything. The wisdom for overdrive is just You alone on auto-drive.

JOURNAL

A Reflection of Your Thoughts

NOTHING TO OFFER, BUT LOVE

As I sit in Your Presence and think so earnestly about my life; I also begin to think about others who have given their lives to You. I ponder how many have given up careers with the highest potential. I thought about some who were making a lot of money in what they did, but these people surrendered everything into Your hands. (You're worth it all.) I then return to thinking about myself, who had none of these things to give up or offer You. The job I had paid pretty well, but nothing to boast about. I do know there had been many failures and many crushing happenings in my life. I really don't feel I knew how to value my life at all behind the mask I was wearing. When I came to You I was mixed up and really didn't know it. Lord, I have been taught so much by The Precious Holy Spirit You gave me. Your wisdom is the best. This world's false wisdom holds you captive until it is ready to present you lost to the god of this world for eternity. The scripture says that You loved us first and You loved us while we were yet in our sins. What was I doing? Chasing after everything that the world presented as gloriously necessary, worth dying for. Many times we're in that "Jones"

> *Because I had nothing to offer You of any great importance, I am now sure that You came after the ability You gave me to love with my whole heart.*

129

syndrome and don't know it. I was also a person who loved people so hard and completely: family, mom, dad, friends, babies and old folks. My aim was to please and help them in any way I could; that is what I freely gave. My love was not agape, but I loved the best I knew how. Because I had nothing to offer You of any great importance, I am now sure that You came after the ability You gave me to love with my whole heart. You ask us to love You with all our hearts, with all our souls, and with all our might. Lord, what I give You is truly not what You are worth, but no one can give You Your worth no matter how they try.

> … We are sure that there is in us nothing that could attract the love of One so holy and as just as Thou art. Yet Thou has declared Thine unchanging love for us in Christ Jesus. If nothing in us can win Thy love, nothing in the universe can prevent Thee from loving us. Thy love is uncaused and undeserved. Thou are Thyself the reason for the love wherewith we are loved. Help us to believe the intensity, the eternity of the love that has found us. Then love will cast out fear, and our troubled hearts will be at peace, trusting not in what we are but in what Thou has declared Thyself to be (A.W. Tozer).

W.O.W. This is profundity, knowing Your love is uncaused and undeserved. Even though I know my love does not weigh in on the scale of YOUR LOVE I shall have no fear, because this audacious love of Yours cast out all fear. My heart, my capacity to love You is still by far the only value I might have to give, I believe You appreciate it, even though it's insufficient. There are those times when we feel we must do more for You, because of all You have done for us. In those times we should give Him what He appreciates most, our love and worship with all fidelity. So, Lord, may You use the only valuable thing I have. O, that my finite love might be pleasurable to You. May every cell in my body recreate itself for the purpose of being consumed in love for You; let every cell in my body jump and excite itself at hearing Your Name in praise. The love that has found us is eternal and secure and only needs us to turn in trust toward Him. Signed: Nothing but love!

SCRIPTURE FOR MEDITATION:

"Many waters cannot quench love, neither can the floods drown it: if a man would give all the substance of his house for love, it would utterly be contemned" (SOS 8:7).

WORD FOR THOUGHT:

Uncaused – *Not caused; being without cause; self-existence (Living Webster Dict. p. 1073, "God is Love.")*

MEDITATE ON:

Your value in God is what He created you for. What may not be a value to one may be of great value to another. Meditate on Your worship, love and adoration and strive to make them your true value to the Lord. Always ponder how you can more perfectly minister this value; for He loves us without any cause of ours. The song by Martha Munizzi came to me, "I was created to make His praise glorious."

RELATIVE PRAYER:

Lord, if there is any way that I can love You more, adore You more, just show me Your pleasure; Lord, remove any failure from my reaching to love You more.

JOURNAL
A REFLECTION OF YOUR THOUGHTS

PERFECT COMMUNING

The day was closing and I was finishing up all the business of the day. I began to feel this most intriguing feeling of joy. It seemed to be increasing every moment. What was going on inside my spirit that caused the release of such a favorable feeling? I thought for a moment and realized it was the expectation of spending time alone with You. You, the One I love, the One I honor, the One who fills my life with Your blessed Presence. My spirit was leaping in joy because of my anticipation of, yes, time alone with You. Everything and everyone has their place in our lives, but You and You alone were capturing my heart with this enjoyable excitement and anticipation.

Just a few days later as I thought on Him and my excitement to be with Him, the Lord revealed to me that this was the work of the Holy Spirit, which had anointed my spirit to draw me into fellowship with Him. He revealed to me that He had been waiting patiently for my attention to turn solely toward Him. I was allowed to discern my spirit anxiously awaiting communion with His Spirit. In a dream He revealed perfectly how He awaits our time and attention: I was busying myself from one room to the next and avoiding one room. I worked all around that room, but eventually I found myself in it, and as soon as I entered, I was caught up in the Spirit and enveloped in a whirlwind with another Person, who I knew was the Lord. I didn't know where I started or where He started, we were so entwined, and He didn't let me go. This was such a powerful dream, and I knew that although I had not been taking time for Him, He was still just awaiting His chance to be with me.

The Lord knows how to perfectly commune His heart to us. Once, I was really wanting to pout, because I had been asking Him for something that I thought would bless the kingdom. In a dream He appeared in a representation I knew was Him, and He knelt before me as I was pouting and just looked at me. I knew exactly what His voice was saying to me, "I am not enough?" Surely I asked for forgiveness. Perfect communing with the Lord is a time when the Spirit whispers those special words from His voice into my spirit, and I voice them out of my mouth. For the most part I know when this is hap-

> *Perfect communing with the Lord is a time when the Spirit whispers those special words from His voice into my spirit, and I voice them out of my mouth.*

pening, because the things I say always amaze and delight. The Holy Spirit has taken control and has given me the words that please the Lord. Perfect communing usually should not be rushed; this peaceful communing can't be known anywhere else, but in Your Personal Presence. I have had people ask me what kind of hobbies I have and they seem to be offended when I tell them that Jesus (Yeshua) is my greatest hobby. (Although I can spend several hours looking for old Christian books at a rummage store.) Lord, I truly enjoy what I have and do with You. Thank you! Sweet Holy Spirit what a wonderful way to spend my leisure, resting in You, enjoying Your voice and feeling what You desire me to feel. There's no place I'd rather be.

SCRIPTURE FOR MEDITATION:

"Blessed (happy, fortunate, to be envied) is the man whom You choose and cause to come near, that he may dwell in your courts! We shall be satisfied with the goodness of your house, your holy temple" (Psalm 65:4 AMP).

WORD FOR THOUGHT:

Linger – *to linger is to remain long or to be slow in going (esp.) from reluctance to depart; tarry, dawdle or loiter, to dwell in contemplation, thought, or enjoyment (The Living Webster Enc. Dict. p. 555).*

MEDITATE ON:

It is only when you rest and linger in Him, that He enlarges the level of His Presence. It will increase until you hear Him speaking for you; what He desires to feel from your heart He Himself stirs up. Then you can perfectly commune with Him. The Holy

133

Spirit will solely promote this special time of communing. The perfection comes from Him Himself.

RELATIVE PRAYER:

Oh Lord! I desire to linger with You. Oh Lord! I desire to please and speak favorable words to You always. Lord, that I might find this place of perfect communing often.

JOURNAL
A Reflection of Your Thoughts

_____

_____

_____

_____

_____

_____

_____

_____

_____

_____

_____

_____

_____

_____

_____

POSSESSION

don't know what You did to cause me to want only You. I don't understand how I came to this place in You, really I don't. I belong to You, I want to belong to You, You hold the reins to my life. My attraction for You over all these years is still growing; I have never felt a decline. Your Person allures me into a continual fascinating wild pursuit. I have such a need to feel Your possession. You possess me in such an exclusively good way that my happiness can only be altered by You. No matter what goes on, this happiness, because of Your possession, will never end. What a profound awareness to know You're walking in me, seeing through me, speaking, using my hands for Your will. The wonderment of a life possessed by You is like having all heaven right here on earth. This kind of relationship keeps you in a wealthy place; you cherish your possession and

I know now the true lasting riches are not in houses, cars and things, but in the possession of Your Person.

you are amazed that somebody like you can possess so much of Him. This is so powerful; the more of You, I possess, the more I know I reflect You. The more of me You possess the more I am like You. I know now the true lasting riches are not in houses, cars and things, but in the possession of Your Person. I know now it is not in rank, position or prestigious places, but in You possessing our person. You are glorious and wondrous; You are the Majestic God of all the universe. Lord, many times I desire to know more and understand more, but then I realize that possibly for now all I need to do is appreciate the beholding I have of

You now. You possess my whole being and I owe You relentless releases of praise and worship for such grace as this in my life.

SCRIPTURE FOR MEDITATION:

"She said distinctly, my beloved is mine and I am His! He pastures his flocks among the lilies" (SOS 2:16 AMPC).

WORD FOR THOUGHT:

Possessed – *(echo) to have; hold; keep (2192) (The New Strong's Complete Dictionary of Bible Words); "Possession" (yere shah) occupancy (3424b) (p. 196); Possession- holding as one's own: ownership: domination, to enter into and control firmly (Webster's Dictionary).*

MEDITATE ON:

This is a place of knowing I am His and He is mine. Believe He will let nothing alter this relationship. There must be a resolve on the inside of you to allow nothing to injure or make obsolete this knowing. Think on and speak often on how good it feels to possess Him in the inner man. He possesses even the very breath you breathe. He is the very breath you breathe.

RELATIVE PRAYER:

Oh Lord, hold my reins firmly.

JOURNAL
A REFLECTION OF YOUR THOUGHTS

_____

_____

_____

_____

_____

_____

WEEK FORTY

MONOPOLY

I t is my heart to make a monopoly of You; just You, day in and day out. At one time I wondered how nuns could repudiate everything for Christ and their ministry to Him. At one time I believed this type of excessive demand could never be for me, but I didn't have a clue of their determined devotion. I now know that the wonder of Your Person leaves very little desire for outside relics. You are the exclusive control of my life. You are the measurement of how everything is arranged or legislated. My worth can be ascertained only through the monopoly You have in my life. You are the commodity to die for, to trade all I have for. I believe that I am exclusively Yours with all rights and privileges at Your disposal. From the top of my head to the soles of my feet, I desire to be totally monopolized by You, as Jesus showed that the Father fully monopolized His life. Then I will know that You will fulfill and finish what you started in my life. This I see does not happen overnight. It takes years of us giving up self and then, to our surprise, giving up self again, to be totally under Your control. The Lord Jesus (Yeshua) says it this way, "If any man come after me, let him deny himself, and take up his cross, and follow me" (Matt. 16:24 KJV). I like how "deny" is defined in the Strong's Dictionary (Greek): to refuse self, to reject self, to disown self, to dispute self. How hard is that? For my life to be monopolized by You, totally powered by You it will take this denying of self. This kind of mental ascent is likened to when a commodity is controlled by one party, or

It takes years of us giving up self and then, to our surprise, giving up self again, to be totally under Your control.

when there is a merger of companies and they monopolize the commodity and have the total power over it. This carries the weight of power the company truly wants. When my life is rendered totally and completely Yours, then I can be sure my life will carry the power to reproduce after Your kind, to Your Glory. More power, all power to You Lord!

SCRIPTURE FOR MEDITATION:

"I am the vine; you are the branches. Whoever lives in me and I in him bears much (abundant) fruit. However, apart from Me (cut off from vital union with Me) you can do nothing" (John 15:5 AMP).

WORD FOR THOUGHT:

Excessive – *Excluding or having power to exclude; limiting possession, control or use to a single individual … etc. –single; sole; also singly devoted; undivided (The Webster's Living Enc. Dict. p. 348).*

MEDITATE ON:

Why he has the right to monopolize our lives. Meditate on His exclusive rights to you, His creation; you, His love child; you, His beloved bride; you, his body and you, His son (spirit-born). You are the one He gave everything for. You are the one the scriptures talk of, "Therefore let no man glory in men; for all things are yours" (1 Corinthians 3:21 KJV). How great is your desire to be even more exclusively under His power.

RELATIVE PRAYER:

Lord have Your own way; You completely control so many of the men and women of God in scripture. People like Anna who never departed from the temple, but served You with fasting and prayer night and day. She was monopolized by You, Lord, what a victory for You, but more so for her. Have Your own way.

JOURNAL
A REFLECTION OF YOUR THOUGHTS

HE'S REAL

Lord, I cherish this ongoing revelation of Your reality. This revelation is so progressive; You lavish us with more and more of Your person, all for the seeking. You said, "Seek and you will find, knock and the door will be opened, ask and receive." When we realize it is not things, promotion or monies we're seeking, but You we seek, we then and only then will find what we can find nowhere else but in You. Lord, You said, "Seek Me with all your whole heart and I will be found of you." In Hebrew, the word "found" means to come forth, appear, attain, to meet or be present, suffice and to take hold on. There are other defining words, but these make us know that God wants to make Himself a reality to us. When our reverence deepens (because of revelation) to the place of knowing we automatically walk humbly and circumspectly before Him. Lord, You are not some kind of distant, unknowable God who can't be approached, neither is that Your desire for Your people. You make Yourself available in all actuality to those who really want to know You, and refuse to put anything before You. The scripture shows us men and women who knew that You would talk to them and appear to them through miraculous ways, There is no questioning or confusion as to whether He's involved in a personal way to fulfill His pleasure in your life. He is truly the life of God.

> From the very first day, we were there, taking it all in—we heard it with our own ears, saw it with our own eyes, verified it with our own hands. The Word of Life appeared right before our eyes; we saw it happen! And now we're telling you in most sober prose that what we witnessed was, incredibly, this: The infinite Life of God Himself

took shape before us. We saw it, we heard it, and now we're telling you so you can experience it along with us, this experience of communion with the Father and His Son, Jesus Christ. Our motive for writing is simply this: We want you to enjoy this, too. Your joy will double our joy! (1 Jn. 1:1-4 MSG).

There was a man who was skeptical of anything that represented supernatural revelation, like encounters, trances and so on, until the Lord took him up into glory and everything changed and he is more excited than ever. (Like the sayings, "the proof is in the pudding" or "a man with learning can't change a man with experience.") This truth about seeking, knocking and asking is profound truth that you will not experience until you get real and pull out all stops. That's when you will encounter His Personal revelation that He chooses just for you. I said personal; all of us are different and because of this He knew what I really needed to know was for real about Him. I'm amazed at how patient

You make Yourself available in all actuality to those who really want to know You, and refuse to put anything before You.

He is to address Himself to us according to our prevailing needs. There are things in scripture that won't become personal to you until He reveals them to you. Some realities won't be felt or understood as they should be until He Himself opens them up to you. Some revelations will make you laugh out loud to know that part of His person. Some things will bring such amazement and cause you just to be in awe, and your respect will heighten.

I know that I was a person who had missed much fathering in my life; my father was not in my life until my adult years. There were many reasons I really needed to know God as my Father; He was ever so kind and gentle to reveal Himself as Father to me. Lord, You knew I needed to know the value and benefits of being secure in a Father's love, and You made me know and understand in a way that revealed You as Abba Father. How Personal can He really be? I realize now that there is nothing that He can't cause you to understand if you're willing to seek the treasure of His Person. He wants to, but we must allow Him to reveal to us the I Am we most need. As a savior, but also a father, friend, mate, mother, lover of lovers, confidante, etc. … Knock, ask, and seek in His Presence, because the treasure house of His Person is inexhaustible. Oh! What my eyes have seen and my ears have heard.

SCRIPTURE FOR MEDITATION:

"Yes, furthermore, I count everything as loss compared to the possession of the priceless

privilege (the overwhelming preciousness, the surpassing worth, and supreme advantage) of knowing Christ Jesus my Lord and of progressively becoming more deeply and intimately acquainted with Him (of perceiving and recognizing and understanding Him more fully and clearly). For his sake I have lost everything and consider it all to be mere rubbish (refuge, dregs) in order that I may win (gain) Christ (the anointed One), ... (for my determined purpose is) that I may know Him (that I may progressively become more deeply and intimately acquainted with Him, perceiving and recognizing and understanding the wonder of His person more strongly and clearly), and that I may in that same way come to know the power outflowing from His resurrection [which it exerts over believers] and that I may so share His sufferings as to be continually transformed (in spirit into His likeness) even to His death, (in the hope)" (Philippians 3:8-10 AMP).

WORD FOR THOUGHT:

Reality – *the state or fact of being real, having actual existence, or having actually occurred; a real thing or fact; that which is real as opposed to that which is imagined or merely apparent; philos; an independent absolute from which all else derives in reality, actually in fact or truth.*

MEDITATE ON:

His Person inexhaustible and how much He wants you to know Him. There are stops you must release to receive the greater reality; ask yourself what they are. Meditate on what He's able to do in your life, what He's able to be in your life, when you believe in all He really is and has become in you.

RELATIVE PRAYER:

Lord, this is my prayer of reality; that I may see You as You are, perceive You and feel Your warmth, touch You and know Your strength, smell You and sense Your fragrance, and feel You and know You're close.

JOURNAL
A REFLECTION OF YOUR THOUGHTS

_____

_____

_____

SNOWFLAKES

In the early morning hours I turned and touched the on button to listen to worshipful music. As soon as the first song began to fill my ears I felt the clouds of love gathering. Drops of love sprinkled over my soul. His love can cover every inch of you in a perfect blanket. Lord, You will carry us into Your banqueting house, and Your banner over us is love, special rewarding love (SOS 2:4). We experience God's love for us when He calls us into His living salvation. There is nothing dead about our salvation, because He lives in our salvation—full of life. Everything becomes alive and vivid in this way of life, love is the true love, joy is real joy, and the peace surpasses understanding. This love is massive and ever so strong and stands amidst all kinds of violations; every onslaught against it doesn't diminish it or stop it from coming for our hearts and souls. This intrinsic love is in the next dimension and goes far beyond our finite measurement of love (so intimate). Although this love is massive and ever so strong, God described it to me one day as being like a snowflake.

The Holy Spirit is all power but is gentle as a dove.

He caused me to envision a snowflake, then to consider all the attributes of a snowflake. He explained that a snowflake is fragile, soft, gentle and tender to the touch. It's pure, exquisite, distinct, purely lovely and rare. Each snowflake is different and distinct; He told me to remember that no two snowflakes are the same. I am to never examine His love for me by comparing it to His love for others. He explained that this relationship must be handled carefully, for it can be insulted and hurt, even though it is strong enough to continue beyond all odds. I know He was telling me not to grieve the Holy Spirit, for He is the One who brings and reveals Jesus (Yeshua) to me. The Holy Spirit is all power but is gentle as a dove. We should handle this love with much care. I know that selfishness, a prideful spirit, being indifferent to His advances toward me or being pre-occupied when He's calling me to time with Him, these all grieve the Holy Spirit. His Words and commands should never be grievous to us when we really love Him. "For the [true] love of God is this: that we do His commands [keep His ordinances and are mindful of His precepts and teaching]. And these orders of His are not irksome (burdensome, oppressive, or grievous)" (1 John 5:3 AMPC). Not honoring the primacy of His inclusive love offends Him, a love so pure, so refreshing, amiable, and so secure. Finding yourself in the efficacy of this love will absolutely change and reset your whole life.

SCRIPTURE FOR MEDITATION:

"I went to sleep, but my heart stayed awake. [I dreamed that I heard] the voice of my beloved as he knocked [at the door of my mother's cottage]. Open to me my sister, my love, my dove, my spotless one [he said], for I am wet with the [heavy] night dew; my hair is covered with it. [But weary from a day in the vineyards, I had already sought my rest] I had put off my garment - how could I [again] put it on? I had washed my feet - how could I [again] soil them? My beloved put in his hand by the hole of the door, and my heart was moved for him. I rose up to open for my beloved, and my hands dripped with myrrh, and fingers with liquid [sweet scented] myrrh, [which he had left] upon the handles of the bolt. I opened for my beloved, but my beloved had turned away and withdrawn himself, and was gone! My soul went forth [to him] when he spoke, but it failed me [and now he was gone]; I sought him, but I could not find him; I called him, but he gave me no answer" (SOS 5:2-6 AMPC).

WORD FOR THOUGHT:

Inclusive – *Comprising, encompassing, embracing; comprehensive; including a great deal, or everything concerned; covering (The Living Word Dict. p. 506).*

MEDITATE ON:

This innate love He has always had for us, awakened in us from its dormant state. Make a vow never again to allow this essential, inherent part of you to sleep dormant again. Your soul surely loves loving Him.

RELATIVE PRAYER:

"O, Lord, thy love is uncaused and undeserved. Thou art thyself the reason for the love wherewith we are loved. Help us to believe the intensity, the eternity of the love that has found us" (A.W. Tozer).

JOURNAL
A REFLECTION OF YOUR THOUGHTS

_____

_____

_____

_____

_____

_____

_____

_____

_____

_____

_____

_____

_____

_____

_____

_____

_____

_____

I DON'T MIND WAITING

Waiting is something we really don't like to do; although when we're waiting on something we believe to be sure and worthwhile, we usually can find the resolve to wait. Lord, why do You hide Yourself or seem to leave us all by ourselves at different seasons in our lives? Yes, because of Your Word I know You're here, but I don't sense or feel you. When we have been made aware of Your Presence, not to feel You brings loneliness and longing with great need for personal fulfillment. Yes, this might sound selfish, but it's true. The determination to wait is never a question, for You are the only one that has the supply that can satisfy the longing and purpose of my life. There is a wonderment to my waiting, for I know when You do appear there is a perfect blessing coming my way, but how will You bestow Your Grace this time? Remembering the many times of waiting, and then remembering the many times You appeared, how engaged it makes me feel; like I could have just won a billion dollars. I usually sense myself back in the Spirit in the high places of Your Presence, the assurances You witness I know are so sound. You have been there all the time. Oh! if those times could last forever. Yes! Everyone who is a true seeker would like to corral You in these times. But You are the Everlasting Spirit and no one can subject You to their space, time and plan. We know we are waiting on the Desire of the Ages and nothing else can suffice. In waiting our souls yearn, our intellect learns the art of stillness and silence, for we know Your thoughts and ways many times are privy only to You, and You expose them as You please. Our emotions are stirred and excited about the prospect that any day You will come to us, our wills actively choose and declare that we will have Your Presence no matter what it costs, no matter the waiting. "I don't think the way you think. The way you work isn't the way I work" (God's Decree). "For as the sky soars high above earth, so the way I work surpasses the way you work, and the way I think is beyond the way you think" (Is. 55:8-9 MSG). Why should we worry or fret when we can't seem to follow You? In those times we don't feel that we are touching Your compassion. Although this can bring an unraveling feeling, this is the time we must touchstone Your Word, and our confident anticipation revives. This is the time to rest and trust in your faithfulness. The Lord gave me an acronym for trust: "To Rest Un Stressed Today." It is an everyday thing to call to our remembrance His Faithfulness. We wait and praise You as David praised You and acknowledge that Your thoughts are precious and numerous toward us; we find encouragement at Isaiah's saying, that we are remembered and as close as the palm of Your hand. I had a dream once where I was looking up toward what seemed like a sports announcer's box where you could see out, but could not see in. I just knew the Lord was up there, but I did not seem to know He was looking at me. I so needed and was trying to get His attention. I was walking backward trying to get a better view. As I was walking back and looking up I walked into my Lord's Loving Arms and I woke up. What a perfect blessing to know His thoughts were toward me as I continued to seek Him in my waiting. This was so real; it's like a virtual reality that takes some moments to come out of. "Cast not away therefore your confidence which hath great recompense of reward for ye have need of patience, that, after ye have done the will of God, ye might receive the promise. For yet a little while, and He that shall come will come, and will not tarry" (Heb. 10:35-37 KJV). "So don't throw it all away now. You were sure of yourselves then. It's still a sure thing! But you need to stick it out, staying with God's plan so you'll be there for the promised completion. It won't be long now, He's on the way; He'll show up most any minute" (MSG). There's a perfect blessing in waiting. You never know how He'll talk to you, or touch you, or reveal Himself to you, but you can trust Him to show up. He won't let your expectation come to naught but will fulfill your every desire in its season.

In waiting our souls yearn, our intellect learns the art of stillness and silence, for we know Your thoughts and ways many times are privy only to You, and You expose them as You please.

SCRIPTURE FOR MEDITATION:

"How precious and weighty also are Your thoughts to me, O God! How vast is the sum

of them! If I could count them, they would be more in number than the sand. When I awake, (could I count to the end) I would still be with You" (Psalm 139:17-18 AMP).

WORD FOR THOUGHT:

Wait *– to stay or rest in expectation, to be in readiness; to remain neglected or be postponed for a time; to remain stationary or inactive in expectation of (Webster's Dictionary).*

MEDITATE ON:

How good you feel in this expectant state. It is a place of faith, where you see spiritually and embrace the thing that you have not beheld naturally. It is where you must enlarge the place of your tent, stretch forth your curtain, spare not, lengthen your cords and strengthen your stakes in preparation. What do you wait for in your encounter? To see His face, His eyes, His voice from the throne, the perfect clarity that comes with oneness in relationship with a new revelation of His Person, remembering everything He has promised and knowing nothing is impossible to those that believe.

RELATIVE PRAYER:

Lord, waiting can be lonely, but it is not passive, for our faith has grasped Your faithfulness and we are energetic and charged. You are faithful to give us encouragement, which keeps us stayed and resting in active expectation. Give us Your encouragement as You did Abram who became Abraham.

JOURNAL
A REFLECTION OF YOUR THOUGHTS

_____

_____

_____

_____

_____

_____

THE VERY THOUGHT OF YOU

Can my heart give You what You want and deserve? Oh! God, I look at the wonders of the sky, the wonders of the oceans and just the waters themselves (streams & waterfalls). I look at the greatness of Your mountains and find myself especially delighted when they are covered with snow (glory). I look at the blending of the many colors on Your flowers, the diversity of trees, Lord! You are so much more elaborate than any word we can use. To feel Your Presence in the movement and wonders of the clouds, which seem to be designed to carry out that assignment. How could man ever doubt Your existence, and why won't they praise You as they behold and enjoy all Your goodness to them? It is in these times that I enjoy just the very thought of You. I'm quickened and aware of just how magnificent and grand You really are. The wonders are ever before us. Truly the heavens declare Your glory and show forth Your expertise; they all speak to us and applaud Your greatness and Your miraculous power (Ps. 19:1-2). Then there are the wonders of life You gave; the way of the beast of the fields, the smallest crawling thing, the order of the birds of the air and the multiplicity of the fish

> *Someone once said, "The angels are constantly saying, 'Holy, Holy, Holy' in Your Presence because they are constantly seeing new revelations of an awesome God."*

in the sea. And of course, man that is fearfully and wonderfully made in the womb. The very thought of you brings warmth to my total being. Lord, just to think on You I have to ask "Who are You, Lord?" The answer comes back, "I Am God." We don't understand what it means to be God and try so hard to rationalize God to something we can comprehend. Your wisdom, knowledge and understanding will astonish the most brilliant of minds; Your determined love for us exceeds the greatest of all love stories ever told. I never dreamt that You could be so personal and revealing as You have been. Will there ever be a time when we will be able to grasp the magnitude of You? Probably not in eternity. Someone once said, "The angels are constantly saying, 'Holy, Holy, Holy' in Your Presence because they are constantly seeing new revelations of an awesome God." Lord, it is beyond my understanding why You should not be everybody's delight; I am then astonished that You want us and allow us to be Your delight.

SCRIPTURE FOR MEDITATION:

"I will meditate also of all Thy work, and talk of Thy doings. Thy way, O God, is in the sanctuary: who is so Great a God as our God? Thou are the God that doest wonders: Thou hast declared Thy strength among the people" (Psalm 77: 12-14 KJV).

"So I will remind myself of Yah's doing; Yes, I will remember Your wonders of old. I will meditate on Your work and think about what You have done. God, Your way is in holiness. What god is as great as God?" (CJB).

WORD FOR THOUGHT:

Wonderment – *wonder; surprise; astonishment; something causing surprise or wonder (The Living Webster Enc. Dict. p. 1144).*

MEDITATE ON:

The wonderment of God, and be amazed concerning what you've seen and heard. Ask God to prepare you to receive all the wonderment He wants to reveal to you. Know there are some places in God we must be prepared to go and they are always His choice for us. Remember the place of Presence and wonderment does have a mutual relationship, or let's just say they run parallel.

RELATIVE PRAYER:

Lord, I pray the prayer of David, Lord, one thing I desire is to look and behold Your Beauty (Psalm 27:4).

JOURNAL
A Reflection of Your Thoughts

_____

_____

_____

_____

_____

_____

_____

_____

_____

_____

_____

_____

_____

_____

_____

_____

_____

I WANT TO MAKE-UP WITH YOU

My Lord and my God, I find myself so many times in Your Presence, when I know You really shouldn't desire to be bothered with me. Really Lord, the last mess up should and could have been avoided, because of all I know I know. Even though I see reasons for You not to show up, You still come with such a forgiving heart; this makes me more ashamed than ever, and I'm saddened for again letting down someone as beautiful, kind and sweet as You. The Holy Spirit has revealed to me the areas that I miss the mark in; these are the areas that I need to watch to be diligent in and pray about. True prayer keeps us more alert and mindful. The word says that Love will cover a multitude of faults. I know that a deficiency in love is the prevailing factor to us coming up lacking in Your sight; We don't have to run away from the law and despise it, for love is what You say fulfills the total law. You informed us by Paul that the law was holy. Lord I do want to be pleasing and holy in Your sight, so I'm back again, asking You to forgive and cleanse me once more. As Your loving, forgiving Presence fills the core place in my heart I always vow in my heart to be more careful, vehemently I affirm to make amends for the sake of Your Name. I fully confess my waywardness and I know I'm fully forgiven, because of Your blood, which is the only way into Your Presence. There is a song that says, "I keep running back to You, and Your arms are open wide. Why did I ever go away?" Why would I allow any kind of distance between the Joy of my salvation, the Fountain of Living Water, You, my Life's Heartbeat. What would happen if You refused to draw nigh to me; this thought is too horrible to think on. I ask myself why You would grace me with this special place of Presence, with my presumptuous ways.

I appreciate the Holy Spirit that alerts me to my misguided ways that offend Your Presence.

David asked You to keep him from presumptuous sin. The Holy of Holies is and forever will be my desired dwelling place. I appreciate the Holy Spirit that alerts me to my misguided ways that offend Your Presence. Oh! How I thank You, Oh! How I praise You, Oh! How I worship You; if this sounds like something that could have been left out of this book you are sadly mistaken. I find myself once more experiencing the vital reconnect with Your Presence. I don't know how others feel, but when my heart condemns me, this in itself becomes a disconnect and I must find the place of repentance. Everything I do without You is simply vainglory. There is an old song that says, "Without You I would be nothing, without You I would fail; without You I would be drifting like a ship without a sail." Lord, You are that Sail. Surely, none would deny Your right to just allow me to drift, but what an amazing God, what an amazing love. Lord, You forgive so freely and give Yourself so freely and copiously. Crying out to You and getting it right with You is such a serious moment. Wow! What a love moment.

SCRIPTURE FOR MEDITATION:

"The Lord hath appeared of old unto me, saying, Yea, I have loved thee with an everlasting love: therefore with loving kindness have I drawn thee. Again I will build thee, and thou shalt be built, O virgin of Israel: thou shalt again be adorned with thy tabrets, and shalt go forth in the dances of them that make merry" (Jer. 31:3-4 KJV).

WORD FOR THOUGHT:

Forgiving – *disposed to forgive; inclined to overlook offenses; compassionate (The Living Webster Enc. Dict. p. 383).*

MEDITATE ON:

It is the goodness and mercies of God that lead to repentance. He never wants us out of His Presence; therefore, the Holy Spirit will always administer conviction that should lead us to Godly sorrow and into true repentance into His loving arms free from condemnation. Oh! how we love His Presence.

RELATIVE PRAYER:

Lord, "create in me a clean heart, O God, and renew a right preserving and stead-fast spirit within me. Cast me not away from Your presence and take not Your Holy Spirit from me" (Psalm 51:10-11 AMP). I need Your Presence of Love.

JOURNAL

A Reflection of Your Thoughts

_____

_____

_____

_____

_____

_____

_____

_____

_____

_____

_____

_____

_____

_____

WEEK FORTY-SIX

NEW SONG

The days we are in have brought forth some of the most heartfelt songs of worship ever. Songs of love that release heartfelt love and adoration to the One who deserves it best. I believe songs of love and desire are a natural occurrence for those who worship the Lord in Spirit and in Truth. Those who find themselves worshiping their God intensely, with great desire for His Presence, will know the creating of the new song, for they are always looking for another way to express their greatest desire and amazement of His Person. The new song I'm talking about comes most definitely from the Holy Spirit. This song possibly will not be published, but will serve a valuable purpose in your life. You don't think this song up; it flows from within, from a certain depth of love and revealed knowledge of Him by the Holy Spirit. Many of these songs are simplistic in nature. The focus of the new song is Him (Jesus); it's about how real, good, powerful, worthy, faithful, holy, lovely, and sweet He is. It's about your experience with His love; the new song comes as an encourager, edifier, and a release of peace to your heart. New songs amazingly can open portals or maintain open portals. We are the Lord's portion and He is our portion; He sends His voice to us through the new song, because we are special to Him in every way. These new songs are songs of degrees; they bring a lifting and anticipation of a visitation with the Lord. They always lift us to heavenly places. The songs of degrees in Psalms (120-134) were songs that led the people up to the Holy city of Jerusalem where

> *His return is imminent, so sing to the Lord a New Song, a passionate song, a song of desire, a longing song.*

the "Shekinah" dwelled. They are called songs of degrees or ascents, because they were ascending up the mountain to the most Holy City to attend the appointed times of the Lord. I believe we all can have an Appointed Time with our Lord as we learn to follow the leading of the Holy Spirit. The Holy Spirit has unctioned these songs that are deeply passionate and intimate. The intimate songs of this time I believe are prophetic and will bring us to the Appointed Time of the soon return of our Bridegroom. I believe these intimate love songs are preparing the Bride for the most intimate time in her life, our meeting with our Intimate Bridegroom. His return is imminent, so sing to the Lord a New Song, a passionate song, a song of desire, a longing song; let His Bride be beside herself for the love of Him.

SCRIPTURE FOR MEDITATION:

"Sing to the Lord a new song, and His praise from the end of the earth! (sing a song such as has never been heard in the heathen world!)" (Isaiah 42:10 AMP).

WORD FOR THOUGHT:

Degrees – *Ma'aleh – elevation, act (lit. a journey to a higher place) Fig. a thought arising, or the condition; a step or grade mark; fig. a superiority of station; spec. a climactic progression (in certain Psalms); things that come up; (high) degree, deal, group, stair, step, story (Strong's Conc., Hebrew).*

MEDITATE ON:

Worshiping in a new song is an elevation, a mounting up to higher places in His Presence. There will be a conjoining in thought and presence. Stay open by faith to a new song that will fill the atmosphere with heavenly presence, which is conducive to a visitation from the Lord.

RELATIVE PRAYER:

Lord, there is a song we sang so often years ago and is still my desire now, "Plant My Feet on Higher Ground." I don't want to live in the mundane, but Lord, I want that higher place of Your Presence, so Holy Spirit, unction me with that new song.

JOURNAL
A REFLECTION OF YOUR THOUGHTS

WEEK FORTY-SEVEN

EXCITED

I have found nothing more exciting than You, Lord. Your Presence has created some of the most exciting times I have ever known. When I lie before You, and entertain Your person, as I lavish myself with that fragrant thought of You, I know I am surrounding myself with an atmospheric indulgence of the delights of the heavenly. My thoughts of You are indeed exciting; the ministry is exciting, but thoughts of You excel every thought. This conjoining is so full of Your (Zoe) life. For lack of a better thought, it's like a battery that has been connected all night to its charger. There is such expectancy; my energy and mind are alert and ready to ascertain from the realm of the heavenly, knowing that I am empowered for anything upon this earth. My spirit man (inner man) is strong and ready to fulfill the mandate of the Holy Spirit; in fact, my whole person has such anticipation, because I am aware of being privy to Your Person, aware that You are really going to receive Your Glory from my life. I remember on one occasion, a young girl named Hunter, about fifteen years old, came to our church. She had come from another church and had wanted the Holy Spirit for some time. She was a foster child and felt that God didn't love her like He did others. God knew her heart was broken. As I took the time to surround myself with thoughts of Him, He gave me a dream about a hunter. As I thought about the dream, I realized He was saying He would give her the Spirit and she would not have to do a thing. When I got to church I was so excited to know I was on a mission for the Lord. I called her up and told her what God said. My middle finger on my right hand began to quiver. So I told her to put her hands up and I touched her only with my middle finger; she immediately went down and began to speak in tongues. Then another young boy, who had been seeking the Holy Spirit for a while, was sent up by his mother. God filled him so powerfully that he didn't stop speaking in tongues for several hours. Wow! That is exciting. I remember lying in His Presence and hearing Him tell me He was going to heal this lady that had cancer at our church. She had not been coming to church every Sunday, because she was very ill. The Lord told me to contact her and tell her she had to be at church that Sunday. When she came, she had no make-up on (totally not her)

Did you know when people see the glory of God they are open to receive the gospel?

she had on a muumuu with house shoes. I had already told her to confess certain scriptures constantly to build faith in His Word. I called her up when the atmosphere of heaven filled the house; we laid hands on her and she went down and God healed her. She went back to the doctor and had tests run; the doctor confirmed she was healed. The doctor commented that he knew it had to do with the cross she was wearing around her neck. By His stripes we were healed. This has been about six or seven years ago. Wow! How exciting. God is always exciting; the things God does (saving and filling with the Holy Ghost, healing the sick and banishing demons) keep the mundane from our services and keep exciting glory resident. Did you know when people see the glory of God they are open to receive the gospel? I really would like to convince you that doing Presence and not just being churchy truly is where the excitement of God is.

SCRIPTURE FOR MEDITATION:

"Now when they saw the boldness and unfettered eloquence of Peter and John and perceived that they were unlearned and untrained in the schools (common men with no educational advantages) they marveled; and they recognized that they had been with Jesus. And since they saw the man who had been cured standing there beside them, they could not contradict the fact or say anything in opposition" (Acts 4:13-14 AMP).

WORD FOR THOUGHT:

Exciting – *calling or rousing into action; producing excitement; thrilling. Stimulation – that which moves, stirs, or induces action (The Living Webster Enc. Dict.).*

MEDITATE ON:

Just being with Jesus makes all the difference in your life. Just spending valuable time with Him turns the plain or mundane life into a joyful, meaningful, and worth filled life. As I saturate myself with His Presence, what will my Jesus do tomorrow?

RELATIVE PRAYER:

Lord, our prayer is to decree and declare Your word back to You, "Therefore with joy shall we draw water out of the wells of salvation. And in that day shall you say, praise the Lord; call upon His name, declare His doing among the people, make mention that His name is exalted. Sing unto the Lord; for He hath done excellent things; this is known in all the earth. Cry out and shout, thou inhabitant of Zion; for great is the Holy One of Israel in the midst of thee" (Isaiah 12:3-6 KJV). We cry and shout for the manifestation of Your Greatness in our midst.

JOURNAL
A REFLECTION OF YOUR THOUGHTS

_____

_____

_____

_____

_____

_____

_____

_____

_____

_____

_____

_____

_____

_____

_____

WEEK FORTY-EIGHT

TALK TO ME

Talk to me Lord, even though Your Logos tells me I am loved, Your Rhema Word to me will inflate my spirit, so that there will be a continual flow of that feeling of being loved. With a Rhema I seem to feel the force of Your love. I can just hear someone's rebuttal, "It's not about feeling," and I do know this. But God is able to be as tangible as you will allow Him to be. Some folks really don't know what our God can show us when we let go and let God be God. Talk to me, Lord, for when You talk to me I feel Your attentiveness and I know Your mind is on me. Talk to me, give me direction, talk to me and say something sweet and all knowing concerning me, something that I know only You could know I need. When You talk to me I am alive, charged, and so supernaturally determined. People can talk to us all day, but when You talk to us personally everything in us comes to attention with anticipation that can't be experienced any other time. My heart yearns for Your voice; that is why I scrabble every day for that special place where You will come in and talk to me. That place in Your Presence; that place of thankfulness, praise and worship; that place of quietness, stillness, and softness; the place to be still and know that You are God. A voice so special that speaks so distinctly and precisely, to each person. We know You are a God who is talking all the time, even when we are not hearing You. We must not be fickle about these times, but be constant in our pursuit, for when we seek to hear Him, we accommodate God's inner voice as we minister, shop, or drive. There are times when I find myself all by myself, but there is no loneliness at these times, just feelings of joy and blessedness in anticipation. For I know it is just You and I, and I talk with You. I talk to You knowing You are there and I anticipate Your Personal voice, a Face to face conversation or that

162

small inner voice. No, it doesn't always happen at that time or moment. You might have me wait until the early morning hours to talk to me. It is always at Your discretion, but that place with You is precious and exuberating. Twice I have heard Your audible voice, which was so distinct and outrageously captivating in every way. It made me feel special and I didn't know how to praise You enough. Why did You do it for me? I don't know, but I will cherish these times for the rest of my days. I remember David's words, "What shall I render to the Lord for all His benefits toward me? [How can I repay Him for all His bountiful dealings?] I will lift up the cup of salvation and deliverance and call on the Name of the Lord. I will pay my vows to the Lord, yes, in the presence of all

Lord I am always yearning to hear from You. I know You will not forget to talk to me.

His people" (Ps. 116:12-14 AMP). You have superseded anything I thought about You, but You talk to me anyway, thrill my little person. Lord I am always yearning to hear from You. I know You will not forget to talk to me.

SCRIPTURE FOR MEDITATION:

"Behold I stand at the door and knock; if anyone hears and listens to and heeds my voice and opens the door, I will come in to him and will eat with him, and he will eat with me" (Revelation 3:20 AMP).

WORD FOR THOUGHT:

Distinction – *not alike, different; separate; unmistakable; well defined; clearly mark off; a mark or feature that differentiates; individual; the quality that makes one seem superior; eminence; a mark or sign of honor.*

MEDITATE ON:

How you feel when the Lord talks personally to you when you know that you know God just spoke to you. It's such a special touch to your relationship. It's like I know I'm unworthy, but wow! You feel special. Then meditate on how personal you feel in your relationship with Him. How you want to get it right. Wow! The light that fills your soul.

RELATIVE PRAYER:

Lord, I pray to hear Your voice always. Your voice is so very distinctive, very strong, precious. It can be humorous, understanding, forceful and consumable in our hearts. Lord, whichever way you speak I want to hear You; for Your voice represents Your love for me.

JOURNAL

A Reflection of Your Thoughts

_____

_____

_____

_____

_____

_____

_____

_____

_____

_____

_____

_____

_____

_____

_____

_____

_____

_____

WEEK FORTY-NINE

HELP ME

Lord help me, I truly want to know that my life in Your Presence is pleasing You to the fullest. Abiding in Your Presence is such a remarkable way to live. I still feel many times I don't know how to receive the abundance of Your Person. Oh! How I appreciate all I have received, but I'm aware that there is yet an overflow I have not experienced that I want to experience. I know that I feel Your fullness many times, but I'm crying for the continual overflow. I don't know if You are able to allow me there, because You know what each of us is able to receive, but if so, I am asking, "What do I do? Is there something I should say? Am I walking in the humility that pleases? Is Your love transparent in all I do?" Lord I never want to offend Your Person and I wonder if I'm even able to dwell in this type of Presence Moses and many of the Patriarchs were privy to. (Although I know and believe from the scripture that we have greater and more precious promises given to us.) Whatever they asked You for, whether the sun standing still or waters congealing; You told Samuel that You would not let one of his words fall to the ground unfulfilled. "And Samuel grew, and the Lord was with him, and did let none of his words

> *I know that everything I give You as a gift must be an accommodation of a heart full of love, gratitude with an abundance of true humility.*

fall to the ground" (1 Sam. 3:19 KJV). Is this kind of relationship available for us today? Is it about sacrifice or about surrender, or about calling? Help me Lord to fulfill all Your destiny concerning me. People who are to appear before royalty take etiquette classes that they may stand before royalty without a clench. There is no one greater than You. Help me, Holy Spirit to appropriate the King of kings with the due worthiness that should be given at His Presence. I realize that my speech and my natural ability are inadequate for One such as You, but I believe I am willing to render what the Holy Spirit is asking for. Then I think I'm really as willing as I believe. I do know I want it so, that is the place where I greatly ask for Your help, Lord. I know that everything I give You as a gift must be an accommodation of a heart full of love, gratitude with an abundance of true humility. After all these years, I am still capable of missing the mark, so I solicit the Holy Spirit's help; I want to give and be what is true and pleasing. Help me!

SCRIPTURE FOR MEDITATION:

"Now when the turn of Esther, the daughter of Abihail the uncle of Mordecai, who had taken her for his daughter, was to come to go in unto the King, she required nothing but what Hegai the King's Chamberlain, the keeper (type shadow of the Holy Spirit) of the women appointed. And Esther obtained favor in the sight of all them that looked upon her ... And the King loved Esther above all the women, and she obtained grace and favor in his sight more than all the virgins; so that he set the royal crown upon her head, and made her Queen ..." (Esther 2:15 & 17).

WORD FOR THOUGHT:

Help – *to be of service, to provide assistance; to contribute aid to; to succor, to relieve, to remedy; to benefit, to promote; to be of use to; to facilitate; to avoid or prevent (The Living Webster's Dict. p. 448).*

MEDITATE ON:

The Holy Spirit is our helper, ask for His assistance always; He knows His position in our lives. Esther didn't really know what was pleasing to the King, so she went to the one who was present with the King all the time and knew his likes and dislikes. The Holy Spirit is forever synonymous with our King and will show us our King's desires.

RELATIVE PRAYER:

Lord, Your word says in John 16:14 that "He (Holy Spirit) will honor and glorify me, (Jesus) because He will take of (receive, draw upon) what is mine and will reveal (declare, disclose, transmit) it to you." Holy Spirit's declaring, disclosing, and transmitting into our lives is the help we ask for. We want You to help us please You. This can't be done any other way. Holy Spirit, thank You for Your needed help.

JOURNAL

A Reflection of Your Thoughts

_____

_____

_____

_____

_____

_____

_____

_____

_____

_____

_____

_____

_____

_____

_____

_____

_____

_____

_____

_____

_____

HOLINESS FELT

Ｔhere are times in Your Presence that Your Holiness (essence of Your Person) becomes a felt experience. God's Holiness in this degree is characterized by sacredness, awe and prostrate reverence. The time I felt this I knew I didn't belong in that place. The Lord Jesus Himself brought me to this place and I perfectly knew I had no right there, but was there only because of Him. His personal self-disclosure; it is an inspiring revelation that touches, and causes a sense of beyond, the influence of celestial holy awe. Natural man can't touch this disclosure. The inadequacy I felt was consistent with scripture, as we read of Daniel's experience, and John on the isle of Patmos. You might ask, "What do you feel in the Presence of felt Holiness?" I really don't know how to explain it, but I'll just say there is an awe that surpasses all awe. You feel it is best not to move unless addressed and you only desire to be clothed upon. You dare not speak, for no one else is worthy to speak. Who He is causes you to react in such reverence and obedience; just waiting on and relying on Him. I never open my mouth to say that I don't belong there; it is like He knows what I'm feeling and He bids me to sit down with Him, and in perfect reverential fear I obey. You feel the mystery of sanctity and sacredness that surpasses your comprehension. It strips you as undone, and you know He is your only source of value. You want to reverence Him above all. I'm not sure it really can be related, but you know you have experienced His Felt Holiness. I have had encounters with the Presence of the Lord and could talk, but not in this one. A.W. Tozer says, "When we are confronted with His Holiness we are brought down and overwhelmed, held (captive) and can only tremble (in fear and reverence) and be silent. (There is) no utterance that can relate." The Holy Spirit knows the mind and heart of God. He knows at any given time what the Father wants to relate at that specified time; sometimes it's love we sense overwhelmingly, at others it's joy or power and we react accordingly and it brings Him pleasure. When He releases a felt holiness it is profundity and abstruseness which overwhelm. Everyone can possibly be privy to this experience, but I'm sure everyone won't be (do not cast your pearls before swine), because being in this kind of Felt Holiness can cause you problems. I believe Peter could relate to being silent when you really don't know what to say. Remember Jesus took only three and was transfigured before them, and Moses and Elijah appeared there. Not knowing what to say, Peter said the wrong thing. A bright cloud overshadowed them and they heard a

> *You feel the mystery of sanctity and sacredness that surpasses your comprehension.*

voice say, "This is My Beloved Son, in Whom I am well pleased; hear ye Him." They were shaking in their boots before Jesus admonished them not to be afraid. The efficacy of the blood of Jesus Christ brings us this nigh to our God. This degree of holiness brings everything in our lives into a prostrate position. Lord, I know this is Your Holiness, which is unattainable, can't be seized or grasped. You have declared us holy and imparted it to us as our "Jehovah M'Qadash," because of the Blood that has been applied to us, "Holiness unto the Lord" belongs to You. All thanks to You for Your unspeakable Gift, Jesus.

SCRIPTURE FOR MEDITATION:

"In the year of King 'Uziyahu's death I saw Adonai sitting on a high, lofty throne! The hem of His robe filled the temple. S'rafim stood over Him, each with six wings—two for covering his face, two for covering his feet and two for flying. They were crying out to each other, 'More holy than the holiest holiness is Adonai-Tzva'ot! The whole earth is filled with His glory!' The doorposts shook at the sound of their shouting, and the house was filled with smoke. Then I said, 'Woe to me! I [too] am doomed! — because I, a man with unclean lips, living among a people with unclean lips, have seen with my own eyes the King, Adonai-Tzva'ot!'" (Isaiah 6:1-5 CJB).

WORD FOR THOUGHT:

Abstruse – *Remote from ordinary minds and notions; difficult to be comprehended or understood; esoteric; profound; recondite, hidden for perception or understanding; obscure (The Living Webster's Dict. p. 5).*

MEDITATE ON:

O! the power of the blood of Jesus. Understand fully that if not for His blood we could never enter into fellowship with our Majestic God and certainly not encoun-ter "Felt Holiness."

RELATIVE PRAYER:

O Father, thank You for the Precious Efficacious Blood of Your Dear Son Jesus. It is the Blood that washes away the tracks of sin that I might enter into Your Holy Presence with genuine humility and holy boldness.

JOURNAL
A Reflection of Your Thoughts

_____

_____

_____

_____

_____

_____

_____

_____

_____

_____

_____

_____

_____

A PLACE OF INTRICACY

Today I awoke, dangled my feet over the side of the bed and began to thank You for strength in my body members. I count it a blessing from You to awake with awareness of Your care for my life and Your constant Presence in my life (wholeness). You are now a part of every part of my life and I want it no other way. Being so aware that not only are You all around me, but also in me. Every fiber, every cell is intricately aware of Your Presence. There is nothing I do, nowhere I go, that I'm not wanting and pleased with my awareness of you. I couldn't think of starting my day any other way then acknowledging Your Good Presence in my life. My awareness of you is continually being heightened through the Holy Spirit's quickening power. We must be excellent stewards of this Life in us; we must meditate, ponder, muse, appreciate and sense You daily. We know the scripture declares You are with us always, but excellent stewardship will bring consciousness to our senses, which brings stimulus and interaction in our daily lives. Our spiritual senses are used regarding an invisible God. David said, "Taste and see that the Lord is good" (Psalm 34:8). The Holy Spirit is the revealer of God; He reveals or gives an awareness of His Presence in diverse ways. It's our stewardship of that awareness that shows us the intricate ways He possesses and keeps our person full with much intentness, desire, and pleasure. The pleasure of His company must be in our heart. It is a known fact that anything you find pleasure in, you do more often. The more often you do it, it becomes habitual and before you know it, it becomes you, what you're know by. Lord, I love you for the awareness that I am in You and You are in me. This is exclusive to me; it is my own personal revelation. People didn't give it, and people can't take it away. It becomes a knowing that will transform your life. The Beloved Lord gives this truth, "Dwell in Me, and I will dwell in you. [Live in Me, and I will live in you.] Just as no branch can bear fruit of itself without abiding in (being vitally united to) the vine, neither can you bear fruit unless you abide in Me. I am the Vine; you are the branches. Whoever lives in Me and I in him bears much (abundant) fruit. However, apart from Me [cut off from vital union with Me] you can do nothing" (John 15:4-5 AMP).

You are now a part of every part of my life and I want it no other way.

The intricate way the Holy Spirit has woven His way into every part and every detail of my life has accrued intimacy at its best. The time that You came in like a vision that I can't explain, Your arm went under my head and brought me into You, I realized at that moment in complete reality that I was in You, but also You were in me. I won't try to explain what happened to me, but the intricacy of it all I will always cherish and never forget. From my rising to my laying my head to rest at night You are there. Even when I'm not aware I'm even in this world You prove You are there. Your involvement in my life through Your dreams and visions that come with an unmistakable touch of the heavenly image, keeps Your reality internalized whether I sleep or wake. So whether awake or asleep You're weaving Yourself into my life. You have so completely entangled Yourself in my life, and it is something I could never completely explain because it is complex to me, and You are the Potter. Older people of God sang a song that said, "Wrapped up, tied up, tangled all up in Jesus." I am amazed and I am astonished; I feel truly there is not a way out of this entanglement and that is such a good thing.

SCRIPTURE FOR MEDITATION:

"That which we have seen and heard declare we unto you, that ye also may have fellowship with us: and truly our fellowship is with the Father, and with his Son Jesus Christ" (John 1:3 KJV).

WORD FOR THOUGHT:

Intricacy – *entangled; involved; difficult to unravel; complicated; difficult to understand- a winding or complicated arrangement; something that is intricate (The Living Webster's Dict. p. 506).*

MEDITATE ON:

Your life that becomes almost oblivious to you, because the life of Christ living in you is so vivid and so obviously what you're all about. Is your life hid in Christ to your amazement? Think on the advantage and the good you have gained by having this arrangement in your life, more aware and more given to Christ living in you, than you're aware of self. He has given us to live in Him from the upper echelon of heavenly places, over our merely human status.

RELATIVE PRAYER:

Lord, overwhelm my person with Your Person.

JOURNAL
A REFLECTION OF YOUR THOUGHTS

_____

_____

_____

_____

_____

_____

_____

_____

_____

_____

_____

A MAGIC CARPET RIDE

Lord, You initiated this flame of love, and I believe my want to experience Your Glamorous Person can never be quenched or put out. It is, I know, perpetual in every way. Forever and a day I desire to behold Your face. This realization of being in Your Presence or experiencing a revelation of Your Person strikes and arouses my being so that I never want this to end. Because of what you have been willing to show me I find myself asking for this "Magic Carpet Ride." I do know what I just said has a lot of whimsy to it. I know this means nothing to most and many will think I'm silly, but you know I know Your ways surpass the norm or mundane Christian thoughts. I say magic carpet ride, because it's like I'm flying around the many times You have taken me so high above the earth; so let me rephrase this to a supernatural carpet ride, maybe many can handle this better. You have taken me above to heights I never could have imagined were possible, above the earth where I could see the world resting on nothing but Your word. You have taken me higher than the moon and stars. On one occasion I rejoiced to see the depths of the sea where the waters bubble up from the floor of the ocean and You told me there is still more. Many would say that's not of God, He wouldn't do that, but what about Paul's adventures into the third heaven, or Ezekiel, and Philip being caught away. If people say it's not of God, then they are saying it is of the devil. Why would the devil give you encounters of God's greatness that cause you to love God more than ever, and search for Him more than ever, and desire to walk up right before Him more than ever? When I encountered these happenings, this beauty and splendor I could only associate with the splendor and beauty of God. It could never be attributed to the devil. It is not something He will do all the time, but when He does, I discern the loving-kindness and goodness of our God that He would reveal these things to a mere human. God really wants us to enjoy Him, enjoy His bigness and His greatness. "I do believe our purpose is to glorify God and to enjoy Him forever" (Westminster Larger Catechism). I have felt His smile and delight, because I was amazed at what He was showing me. I can't say what the criterion is to encounter Him this way, but to love Him with all the power you possess. I'm sure seeking Him is the definite positive and hasn't hurt. Surely these encounters and pleasures are not because of anything great in me, but the simple fact I love and will deny myself and give anything for His Presence

> *God really wants us to enjoy Him, enjoy His bigness and His greatness.*

might carry some weight. Salvation is the greatest thing You have for us, Lord, but when we value our salvation with great joy more than life itself, when we value and think more of the One who gave it, more than anything else, then You are so ready to reveal to us Your Majestic Splendor. "The person who has My commandments and keeps them is the one who [really] loves Me, and whoever [really] loves Me will be loved by My Father, and I will love him and reveal Myself to him [I will make Myself real to him]" (John 14: 21 AMP). Oh! There is so much more of Our Magnificent God to be had, take the many unnecessary limits off and aspire to have it all.

SCRIPTURE FOR MEDITATION:

"God can do anything, you know — far more than you could ever imagine or guess or request in your wildest dreams! He does it not by pushing us around but by working within us, His Holy Spirit deeply and gently within us" (Ephesians 3:20 MSG).

WORD FOR THOUGHT:

Aspire – *to breathe (in expire, respire, etc.), to endeavor after; to desire with eagerness; to aim at something elevated or above one; to be ambitious (followed by, to or after); to ascend; to tower, to point upward; to soar (The Living Webster's Dict. p. 59).*

MEDITATE ON:

God is glamorous. To know God is to romantically aspire after His glamour. One of our songwriters expresses that He has become the very breath I breathe. How desperate are you for your next breath of His glamour?

RELATIVE PRAYER:

Lord, my terminology of a "Magic Carpet Ride" will probably confuse some, but You, Lord, know and You are familiar with all the thoughts of my heart. You know it well. You know I am asking for those special times I have had with You; exclusive fellowship, closeness and togetherness that I believe you are willing to give all Your children. I want more! (Jeremiah 33:3).

JOURNAL
A Reflection of Your Thoughts

_____

_____

_____

_____

_____

_____

_____

_____

_____

_____

_____

_____

_____

_____

CONCLUSION

This concludes 52 weeks of devotionals in His Presence. I know for most of you that are hungry for more you consumed the devotionals as quickly as you could and that's wonderful, but go back and assign a devotional of His Presence for each week on the calendar year and take time to reflect. (This is so important.) I am sure these will keep your heart full of the warming effects of loving Him exclusively; there will be times that your passion will turn into a fiery blaze that can only be quenched by spending x amount of time in His Beautiful Presence, just you and Him. Presence is very uncomplicated: you just need desire. This quote is from A.W. Tozer (*Men who Met God*): "What I am anxious to see in Christian believers is a beautiful paradox. I want to see in them the joy of finding God while at the same time they are blessedly pursuing Him. I want to see in them the great joy of having God and yet always wanting Him!" Every Christian who has learned to love Christ back should desire to enter into a deeper more captivating relationship with the Lord through praise, worship, sacrifice, service and just spending time with our heart's Desire. Many Christians who live in the mundane and are still vacillating between the outer court and the world will never really accommodate the place of the Holy of Holies, although they've been bidden to come. Their captivation is not with the face of Jesus, but with more of this world's goods, or with position and prestige in Christendom. So, heartbreakingly, they only want to see His hand. I truly believe that all the true riches in all areas are to be had only by seeking His face. Today I know there is a wealthy place (treasure unbeknown to many Believers) where you can have all you can accommodate. There is an old song that we sing as God prompts when we're making an altar call, "Come to Jesus, come to Jesus, come to Jesus, right now, for He will save you, for He will save you, right now." I bid you also through the prompting of the Holy Spirit, to keep on coming and not stop at salvation. Don't allow yourself to plateau, but keep coming; want to see and experience the Face of your Beautiful Savior. He will accommodate you. "Call to Me and I will answer you and show you great and mighty things, fenced in and hidden, which you do not know (do not distinguish and recognize, have knowledge of and understand)" (Jer. 33:3 AMP). God does want to show us His Greatness; His hidden treasures that are fenced in and inaccessible to those that don't have time to live in His Face. Encounters that reveal His Person, encounters like Ezekiel and John had, will always produce a greater level of humble worship. He can still bring you up into the heavenly. I truly know that desire, passion, godliness, and a needy spirit (broken and contrite spirit) will bring true encounters with the Holy One, never ever to be forgotten. Listening for the times when God wants to talk to you, learning and being aware of His Presence is a door opener to encounters. You will esteem and cherish every encounter with Him. You will find that if you continue seeking His Presence above all that this pleasurable grace from the Holy Spirit will keep you from stopping.

Every Christian who has learned to love Christ back should desire to enter into a deeper more captivating relationship with the Lord through praise, worship, sacrifice, service and just spending time with our heart's Desire.

I have truly enjoyed writing about some of my memories of His Presence in my life. As I said before, I didn't really know if this was from the Lord and struggled with some of the revelations; first, because I knew some were my intimate personal encounters with God, but He gave me that dream that caused me to believe it was Him. I awoke with not a complete understanding of the dream, until I began to question myself about writing this book of memoirs and He brought the dream to my remembrance. So the dream I had a while ago assured me this was of the Lord. How smart and wise is our God. Second, many religious Christians have limited God to the point that the only supernatural happenings they will believe are in the Old and New Testament (if they really believe them). Everything else sounds like witchcraft or they give all credit of the supernatural to the demonic. I love this passage of scripture that is so intriguingly informative, "Now unto Him that is able to do exceeding abundantly above all that we ask or think, according to the power that worketh in us" (Eph. 3:20 KJV). The Lord has truly revealed to me that He is the same yesterday, today and tomorrow. "There should be this consistency that runs through us all. For Jesus doesn't change—yesterday, today, tomorrow, He's always totally Himself (Heb. 13:8 MSG). The trueness of a personal relationship with Him has exceeded everything I could have thought was possible. If you can only believe what you think possible, you have not locked into the true, infinite God. A.W. Tozer says that Paul teaches that God can be known only as the Holy Spirit performs in the seeking heart an act of Self-disclosure. The yearning to know What cannot be known, to comprehend the Incomprehensible, to touch and taste the Unapproachable, arises from the image of God in man's nature. Deep calleth unto deep, and though polluted and landlocked by the disaster mighty theologians call the Fall, the soul senses its origin and longs to return to its Source. How can this be realized? The Bible's answer is simple: "through Jesus Christ our Lord." He says that "In Christ and by Christ, God effects complete Self-disclosure, although He shows Himself not to reason, but to faith and love. Faith is an organ of knowledge, and love an organ of experience. God came to us in the incarnation; in atonement He reconciled us to Himself, and by faith and love we enter and lay hold on Him" (*The Knowledge of the Holy*). The Holy Spirit is the revealer of Him who made it all. "When asked in reverence and their answers sought in humility, these are questions that cannot but be pleasing to our Father which art in heaven" (A.W. Tozer).

I believe these 52 weeks of devotionals have been literally drawing you into a tangible Presence that impresses on your heart relationship. The remarks from the ones who have read this devotional were that they had to take some praise breaks, because Holy Spirit Presence filled their space tangibly. I pray as you read you experienced a heightened desire to spend quality and quantity time before the Lord. As you read and contemplate this devotional you will have been provoked to engage in the mandate of Jesus to seek, ask, and knock. This devotional was truly meant to co-labor with the Holy Spirit, to stir every slumbering desire into revival. Those who are already passionate and full of fervor, you won't just stop at the throne room, but as Esther found herself in His chambers, you also will go after the true place of intimacy. Everything you want and everything you need is right there. Always return to your journal and release your thoughts, prayers, declarations, revelations; add more as they come to you; they are invaluable. I have learned over the years you will never regret writing them down. These writings act as a gauge and a prompter in your growing love for God. There are things you will experience that I'm sure this book will open your spirit to receive, because faith comes by hearing. "Believe in the Lord your God, so shall ye be established; believe His prophets, so shall ye prosper" (2 Chron. 20:20 KJV). There are things you will experience, that can never be truly spoken or explained as you would like and then some things, just meant for His intimate "face to face" friends, are never to be spoken. Be very mindful of the Holy Spirit, for the Holy Spirit is the way to look into Him and see. I know the Lord is telling me to make you know if you came with your heart open and at liberty there is a Divine revelation for you. The desire for perfect intimacy will be fulfilled.

PASTOR PATRICIA WHEATON'S BIO

Pastor Patricia Wheaton is the founder of New Life Christian Church in Ontario, California. Pastor Wheaton holds a Bachelor's degree, a Master's degree, and a Doctorate in Ministry. Pastor Wheaton is also the founder of Beyond the Veil School of Ministry, which is now known as Jaddai Bible College, located in Ontario, California, where the emphasis is on the deeper revelation of Christ through scripture.

Pastor Wheaton loves her beautiful family and loves God with all her heart and has a burning desire to minister to His people.

IF YOU'RE A FAN OF THIS BOOK, WILL YOU HELP ME SPREAD THE WORD?

THERE ARE SEVERAL WAYS YOU CAN HELP ME GET THE WORD OUT ABOUT THE MESSAGE OF THIS BOOK...

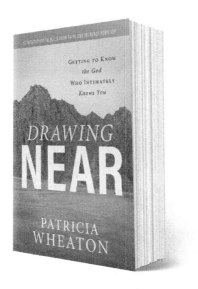

- Post a 5-Star review on Amazon.
- Write about the book on your Facebook, Twitter, Instagram, LinkedIn – any social media you regularly use!
- If you blog, consider referencing the book, or publishing an excerpt from the book with a link back to my website. You have my permission to do this as long as you provide proper credit and backlinks.
- Recommend the book to friends – word-of-mouth is still the most effective form of advertising.
- Purchase additional copies to give away as gifts.

The best way to connect with me is by email: pastorpwheaton@gmail.com.

www.pastorpatriciawheaton.com

BEYOND THE VEIL
SCHOOL OF MINISTRY

P.O. Box 4195

Ontario, CA 91761

pastorpwheaton@gmail.com

Made in the USA
Las Vegas, NV
09 January 2021

15574850R00108